Blowing the Whistle

BLOWING THE WHISTLE
A Referee's View of Soccer

Dirk Baay

Halftime Press
Colorado Springs, Colorado

Blowing the Whistle
A Referee's View of Soccer
By Dirk Baay

ISBN 0-9656463-0-0

Copyediting and design: Georgia Shepherd Maas
Illustrations: Flint Whitlock
Cover Design: Ted Yun

Photos on pages 7, 15, 21, 27, 47, 61, 73, 89, 105, 117 by Flint Whitlock
Photo on page 1 courtesy of Tutt Library, Colorado College
Photos on pages 83 and 95 courtesy of El Paso Pride Soccer Club, Colorado Springs

Halftime Press, P.O. Box 383, Colorado Springs, CO 80901-0383
Fax: 719-389-6214

Printed in the United State of America

TABLE OF CONTENTS

Preface

I GREW UP IN AMSTERDAM NOT FAR FROM THE STADIUM of Ajax, one of the most famous soccer clubs of our era. When I was six or so, on a walk with my father I suddenly charged into a group of men playing soccer and kicked the ball away from the goalkeeper amidst laughter and applause. That was the beginning of my undistinguished career as a player. It was also the start, however, of my lifelong passion for soccer as a spectator and a coach and as a referee for more than thirty years.

It is from that broad experience that I have written this book which is not only about refereeing, but also about other aspects of the game. The first chapters deal with the referee's main task of calling the game according to the *Laws of the Game* established by FIFA (Fédération Internationale de Football Association) and the appended "Decisions of the International Board."* I want to talk freely about the laws themselves and about the spirit of the laws that must govern their application. The book deals in large part, however, with the interactions among the people who play the game, those who watch it, and the men and women with whistles who mediate what goes on. The final section addresses new developments in the game such as the miraculous growth of youth soccer and women's soccer in our generation, as well as other changes and challenges that lie ahead.

---

* These documents have been printed at the end of this book with the permission of FIFA.

My talking freely means that everything in this book comes from my own experience and observations. It does not carry the official approval of any organization. Also, it is not meant for the referees at the top, but for those who spend much of their free time in the city parks and on high school and college fields working their hundred or more games a year. I belong to that category, which explains some of the things I have to say and the way I say them. Some of my friends and colleagues may raise an eyebrow here and there, but I trust that in most cases they will agree with my views. I am grateful for the useful suggestions many of them have made for this book, though naturally they are not responsible for the final product. I am especially indebted to my good friends Dick Burns and Jim Hattersley. My profoundest thanks go to my editor and designer, Georgia Shepherd Maas, and illustrator/photographer Flint Whitlock, without whom this book would never have been published.

I also thank the thousands of players and coaches who have let me know on the field when I was wrong. And how! This book is also for them. It may give them a better sense of what our job is and why we treat certain situations in ways that seem to them questionable. We have one thing in common: we all love the game of soccer, whatever our roles as players, coaches, or referees. The mistakes we make are the result of ordinary human weakness and occasional blindness.

This book is not just about soccer. It is also about life. What happens on the field is the mixture of human excellence and failure from which no actor in this drama — including referees — is exempt. In that sense, we are all, referees and even spectators, players of the game. You are invited to join me in this adventure.

Introduction

REFEREEING IS AN ART. PRACTICING THAT ART IN whatever sport you choose is one of the best things you can do with your leisure time. It lets you remain close to the sport you love. For me, soccer was my first love, the one you never get out of your system. Refereeing is healthy and wholesome for body and soul, and you can do it practically for a life time. Kept in the right perspective, it will not interfere with your primary roles in life, your profession, your family, and your community. Rather, it will benefit them because refereeing will add to your own growth as a person.

Refereeing makes you a member of a wonderful fraternity of people who share this avocation and who are as dedicated as you are. They are a source of support and strength when things are tough, on or off the field. I have had colleagues who at one time or another quit because they could take it no longer but who have come back to become mainstays and leaders in our state association of referees as well as on the national level. Being active in soccer has sustained me at difficult times in my life. Soccer was always there to perk me up with its vibrant life, comradeship, and infusion of energy because it demanded energy.

In listing all these good things that refereeing soccer can do for a person, we must not forget what is central to being a referee. It is the contribution one can make to the lives of others, especially to young people who need the mixture of freedom and discipline that sports demand, the teamwork, the wholesome outlet for their energies, and the guidance of adults who care about the right things. We do not need medals and we should not expect any. The feeling that we have contributed something of value in this unique way should be enough.

The job is never finished of course. Like all jobs, reffing has its routines, the things that don't change and that you should always feel confident about. By the same token, reffing also brings changes and challenges, new things we have to learn that may tax our imagination and our courage to the limit. As I said in the Preface, sports parallel life. Life is serious but it is also a game that we have to learn to play well if we are to enjoy it and thrive. Through sports we can learn the skills required in handling all our other business: the strategies and tactics for success, the nurture of human relationships, and the art of giving and taking in the right proportions. Refereeing can teach you the art of being yourself with pride and humility, and of assessing your own strengths and weaknesses. Finally, refereeing offers us an opportunity for learning the most difficult thing of all: to love and honor the right things for their own sake, with loyalty and steadiness.

How I Got Started

I began refereeing in the early 1960s, when American soccer was about to begin its rapid growth. There was a serious dearth of experienced referees then, just as there is now. Some of us got into reffing in those days because we had had playing experience elsewhere while the American heartland still thought of soccer as a foreign sport. In some areas, of course, there was a good deal of high school and college soccer, especially in the East and in a few other hotspots such as St. Louis. There was also club soccer in virtually all metropolitan areas with large immigrant populations. The USSFA (U.S. Soccer Football Association), as the national association was then called, always entered national teams in qualifying rounds for the World Cup and the Olympics. In some years these teams even played in a final round, mostly with indifferent success, except for the dramatic American victory over mighty England in the World Cup of 1950.

Apart from such great efforts by small bands of dedicated players and officials, American soccer went largely unnoticed. There was as yet little organized youth soccer that could have provided the breeding ground for soccer at higher levels as it does now. Large universities such as my alma mater Michigan, with its wealth of sports programs, grudgingly allowed student clubs to use a wellworn practice field with football goals. Players paid for everything themselves. There were few paid soccer coaches, let alone scholarships. The first national collegiate championship for men was played in 1959 and won by St. Louis University. Women's soccer? With a few exceptions, it was not even a gleam in anyone's eye. How things have changed!

Growing Up Fast

The statistics below point to dramatic growth, especially in youth soccer.

	1974/75	1985/86	1994-95
Registered adult players	NA	104,000	175,000
Registered youth	103,432	1,229,000	2,390,000

Once the soccer ball really started rolling everywhere, with new clubs being formed and more high schools adding soccer, the recruiting of new referees became crucial. Many newcomers without soccer experience taught themselves by studying FIFA's *Laws of the Game* as well as the High School Federation's and NCAA's private variations on the international rules. There were few clinics for referees, so most of us were on our own.

I was pressed into service as a soccer referee in Iowa in the early sixties, when some of the private colleges in the Midwest Conference began to organize club teams. The local college coach, a volunteer himself, gave me an NCAA rule book the day before my first game, and I went to the store and bought a striped shirt and a whistle. There was no other organized soccer far and wide.

After a year in West Africa, where I coached and refereed some soccer in 1964, I moved to Colorado. There, a real soccer community existed. Denver had an established amateur league led by the Denver Kickers, and the well-organized Rocky Mountain Intercollegiate Soccer League was beginning to flourish under the leadership of Dr. Joe Guennel. As yet, no distinction was made among Divisions I, II, and III. Some good soccer schools competed in the NAIA (National Association of Intercollegiate Athletics), in which Denver University was a national soccer power. There, in the fall of 1966, little Colorado College, with some 1,200 students, played in an NCAA play-off round against St. Louis University, then the almost perennial national NCAA champions. Now, thirty years later, both men's and women's collegiate soccer enjoy a system of regional playoffs in all three divisions and a "Final Four" weekend to crown a national champion.

During that renaissance of soccer, schools and colleges generally used the deficient two-man system of control. Most amateur games had only one certified referee and used club linesmen. I remember some of these linesmen as running (or walking) the line with the flag in one hand and a beer in the other after having played themselves in the previous game. By the early 1970s things began to improve rapidly. The USSF began to pay more attention to referee development. Some people sought to become certified as referees in a sport they had never played themselves. Others volunteered as coaches. We cannot sufficiently emphasize what the sport of soccer owes to these newcomers. Many of them had never seen a high-level soccer game or had a chance to work with experienced colleagues, so they had to start refereeing "by the book." Most of them were dedicated and learned fast. Now, twenty-five years later, we are still working hard to raise the numbers and competence of referees to keep pace with the growth and improvement of play at all levels. Hats off to all the pioneers in local and state soccer organizations. Without them we would not be where we are today.

Blowing the Whistle is, particularly in the first part, a clinic in book form for active referees as well as for others who have a keen interest in questions of rules interpretation and refereeing practices. After "Halftime" we go on to discuss broader aspects of refereeing such as recruitment and organization, as well as the growth of soccer in the United States and some of the problems and opportunities attendant upon that growth that are of special interest to referees.

Ancient drawings show that perhaps as early as 1600 B.C., a game called *tsu-chu*, meaning kick-ball, was played in China. A thousand years later, the Japanese played a game called *kemari* that may have been similar. The sixth-century Greeks had a game called *episkyros,* and the Romans played *harpastum,* but in all likelihood such games involved both kicking and carrying the ball. The Romans took their game to Britain, where, as legend has it, sometime during the third century the people of the town of Derby beat the Roman soldiers at their own game and continued the game using their skulls. Such stories may be apocryphal, but clearly these forms of football were not for the faint of heart.

1

Getting Out of the Way

I N SPORTS, AS IN MOST OF LIFE, THERE HAVE TO BE RULES. You can't play tennis without a net. And wherever life and sports are taken seriously, there are people who enforce the rules. In life they are judges, in sports they are called umpires or referees. They see to it that all participants may be assured of the three basic things we look for: fairness, safety, and satisfaction. For me, the objectives in sports are very much like the opening clause of the Declaration of Independence when it states that all people are created equal and that as such they have an inalienable right to "life, liberty, and the pursuit of happiness." That's what we seek in soccer too. All players have a basic claim to fairness (equality), safety (life and liberty) and enjoyment (the pursuit of happiness).

So we referees are the judges who should see to it that there is a level playing field for everyone, that no one gets hurt, and that everyone has fun. That "having fun" applies to the referee also. A referee who approaches the game as a confrontation and a test of his* ego had better hang up his whistle. Neither he nor the players are going to enjoy themselves. Referees are important, but not as important as the players. They can play without a referee if need be, as they did in the old days in England when "gentlemen" played against each other and were their own umpires. Those days are long since gone, but I like to think that in most sports there is a bit of that spirit left. It happened to me once that the time of an adult men's game had been changed without the referees having been notified. When I arrived at the field, the game had been underway for some time, with players calling their own out-of-bounds and offsides, and even fouls. Although without a referee the result could not be official, they were doing just fine! That changed when I took over: they began to play a lot harder. Now they did not need to police themselves anymore. They had me to do it! The lesson in this is: we referees are important but not indispensable.

Referees are there to keep order, but they are not policemen who run around with a drawn gun in the shape of a whistle and blast away with it whenever they think someone "done wrong." Referees who think and act that way should stay home. Actually, the good police officers I know are more like good referees than like Wyatt Earp. Unfortunately, there are referees who come to the park as if they were entering a battlefield. They are the generals. They bark battle orders to their linesmen — if

---

* Throughout most of this book masculine pronouns are used for referees, players, and coaches in order to avoid the awkwardness of constant "his or her" references.

they pay attention to them at all. And they have little respect for the players. Any questioning of a call produces a card, and they sense the possibility of evil in every move a player makes. My advice to such referees is:

> *Change your act and get out of the way!*

First Impressions

Do you know what impression you make? It starts with the way you enter the field. Are you on time, early enough to handle the preliminaries in a calm and orderly way? Are you dressed impeccably (and, if you're a man, shaved)? If you have to check in the players, do they get a sense that you are looking forward to the game as much as they are? Show respect for them, and you will get it in return. If they know you well and you have previously established a good relationship with them, you may loosen up a little and be less formal. But avoid giving the impression to the visiting team that you are a friend of the home team. That applies also to your relationship with coaches and other team personnel.

Coaches

At higher levels of the game there is generally no need for a referee to talk with coaches at all. But at the levels at which the majority of us work games, in local settings, it is expected that you introduce yourself to them and perhaps briefly discuss questions of overtime and substitution, the condition of the field, or other things you cannot take for granted. If you take a few moments to chat with a coach before the start, it may help in getting cooperation during the game. However, if you talk to coach A during the warm-up, be sure to talk also to coach B. Show them that you care about safety. If there is a bad sprinkler hole on the field or if something is wrong with a player's equipment, talk to the coach. But keep it brief. If you have to keep a player from participating for lack of a playing card or because of a cast, don't argue about it.

Assume that a coach knows the rules and does not need a long explanation. If you are sure that you are right (and you'd better be!), don't go for your rulebook and show him what it says on page 13. Never interrupt a game because the coach wants to speak to you, unless he has called the linesman about something that needs attention, and the linesman in turn signals you. That "something" cannot be the call you just made or the goal you allowed! Once the game has started, it belongs to the players. The only footnote to this is the tradition in American school and college sports that the coach has a limited right to be heard. This is not the case in soccer under USSF and FIFA auspices: referees deal directly with players and captains. Technically, a coach cannot even take out of the game a player who refuses to leave, or change the captain's choice at the coin toss.

Loosen Up

Show a sense of humor, but don't tell jokes. If you slip and fall down and all the players laugh (they will), laugh with them. But don't laugh when they slip! Let them have their egos and hide your own. If a dog runs onto the field, don't bark, "Whose dog is that? Get him off the field!" Rather, see what you can do to help and ask the owner to hold on to the beast.

At the coin toss, do not tell the captains, as I heard a referee say recently, "I'm not going to stand for any talking. If you captains have a question, you can ask me, but not to complain about a call I made. You understand that?" This referee is not showing how tough he is. He may

be showing his own insecurity. And the players know it! Also, do not refer to any previous trouble you may have had with this team, or that another referee reported. Every game is a new game.

Generally, do not address players by their names unless you know them well. In Munich once in 1972 — I was very close to the sideline — I did hear a referee say to the great Franz Beckenbauer, "Please, Mr. Beckenbauer, stop whining." It worked, but generally you ought to ignore a player's identity. Be stern, but not vindictive. Be friendly, but not chummy. I always thought that my old friend Artie Wachter, a FIFA referee some time ago, and still active today, had a good folksy way of calling college players "son" as in, "Hey there, son, let's cut that out." But when I used it with a high school player, the fellow turned around and said angrily, "I'm not your son!" All I could say was, "You're right, and I'm not your father. Just don't do that again." I could have said, "Thank God you're not," but would that have helped the situation? It also taught me again that what works for one referee does not always work for another. Be yourself! Be there, but know when to disappear. That is what I mean by "getting out of the way." Don't ever be a stumbling block. It's *their* game!

Look the Part

Referees are judged 50 percent by the calls they make and 50 percent by the way they carry themselves. In assessor reports for upgrading referees, the referee's bearing is an important criterion: "How well did the referee control the game overall? Was he able, by virtue of his personality, to command respect and have authority?" I watched the 1994 World Cup games with special attention to the referees. I hope you did too. I am sure that you disagreed with some of their foul calls and offside calls, as did I. But I admired their appearance, their fitness, and their quiet, self-assured manner. I saw one referee push a player out of the way when he tried to keep him from carding a teammate, but he was not aggressive. I did not see any referee looking at players or to the bench for their reaction to a call, which is what insecure referees do. If you do that, players or coaches will be sure to let you know what they think. You always get what you ask for! What it amounts to is that you are creating an impression and must make sure that it's a good one. It will help you when you have to make difficult decisions.

Getting Respect

To get respect, you have to show respect for the players. I had a colleague who, whenever a high school player complained about something, would reach in her pocket and give him a candy pacifier. That's the wrong kind of humor. The age of the players and the level of play may make a difference in certain ways, but your respect has to be there at all levels of the game. Don't shake your head when someone misses an easy goal, as if that never would have happened to you. Be positive, but stay out of the game as much as you can. Some of us are by nature more flamboyant, but I think we admire most the referee who is quiet, crisp and confident, and does the job, no more and no less. God made all kinds of referees, but nobody likes a wimp or a bully or a clown!

Know Thyself

There are as many styles of refereeing as there are personalities. You have to know your own personality so you can take advantage of your good qualities and keep your weaknesses to a minimum. If you tend to be loud, tone it down. If you tend to be too serious, try to take yourself a little more lightly. If you are apt to make rash decisions, take your time, even if it's only a second. Some of us have worked hard at learning the game but have not spent much time working on ourselves. When I look at the top referees, I find that they are not much better at judging plays than most of us.

They miss some calls, as all of us do. But they excel in their deportment, their disposition, and their composure. They sell themselves not only by what they do, but just as much by what they are.

I have often told young players to watch soccer on TV because they can learn a lot about rules application that way. I would make the same suggestion to referees. Watch referees at international soccer games, and also referees in other professional sports that have a lot of speed and contact, with different styles and changes of flow, like hockey and basketball. How do they "work" the game and the players? What do they call, and what do they let go, and how do they adjust as tension grows and tempers rise? They are not at the top by accident.

Good referees don't get respect. They earn it!

2

Reading the Game

R EADING THE GAME AS SPECTATORS, COACHES, AND REF-erees is one of the pleasures of watching sports. We develop an aware-ness of the ebb and flow of the game, of its rhythms and of the way its pieces fit together to make up the whole. In soccer, those pieces are the formations a coach chooses or the way the players carry out their special assignments for guarding, for their set plays, or for organizing an offside trap. It may be the overall strategy of a team that changes as the game goes on, like playing more offense or defense depending on the play of the opponent, the weather, and the score. Almost certainly, these strategies will have an effect on how the referee calls that game or positions himself; he too has his strategies. At all times referees should be aware of what they are doing and why.

Don't Call What You See!

This may sound strange, but it is just another way of saying that referees' choices are never automatic. They do not have an electronic checklist in their minds that lights up at item number 54 the moment it gets a visual impulse: "Foot trips player — whistle — direct free kick" or "Blue 13 played ball after whistle — whistle again — warn player — resume with original call." Referees who are programmed robots have no business on a soccer field. Do not simply call what you see. Call what you must!

Will It Help the Game?

The real sequence goes through your mind like lightning: "Look at that — was it intentional — did the forward loose the ball? — what happens if I call it, what if I don't? — will it help the game?" That is the most important question. What are this game's needs at this particular time? No two plays are ever alike because every play is part of a different game or a different context. How different? Consider this sequence flashing through your mind: "... the weather is getting worse — there's a lot of slipping and sliding — but these are fourteen-year-old girls, light as a feather — yeah, but they can get hurt too — but this is a tournament final, give them a chance to finish — now that striker goes down — her coach is going bonkers — clamp down a little — watch for lightning — how much time left? — whistle for the trip — say something to that fullback — no wall? if they're ready, let them take the kick — look at the linesman — he raises the flag for offside — ah, the ball goes over the bar — wave him off — goal kick ..." That sounds rather breathless, but it's a very ordinary scenario flashing through your mind. Yes, things happen fast, but that's what you are there for, making quick decisions and living with them. If you make a mistake, you can mull it over tonight while you lie awake. Should I have . . . ? "Uneasy lies the head that wears a crown," said Shakespeare. What crown? A little plastic whistle is all I've got! Sorry, fellow, it'll have to do. Try again tomorrow.

Whether or When

A good referee has experience in reading the game, so he senses what the tone and the flow of the game require of him. Remember, he is playing the game too! He has to decide when he should sprint as fast as he can to follow the attack and when he should hold back slightly because the other team is known for good defense and launching fast counters. Throughout the game he makes hundreds of large and small decisions beyond the foul calls and the out-of-bounds calls:

♦   whether he should look back over his shoulder to watch the two players who have collided before;

♦   whether to allow fairly physical play because the flow of this game is good and fast, OR whether to start tightening things down — the score is still tied . . . how to combine fast play with safety;

♦   whether to jump in and simply talk to those players chesting each other while play is stopped, or whether to card them — what will be most effective;

♦   whether to overplay one end of the field a bit because there is one young, inexperienced linesman who may need to be overruled on occasion (just remember to explain and thank him later);

♦   when to clamp down on the four-letter frustration words flying around . . . I'm not hard of hearing, but I don't have to hear everything, right? — there are enough other things that need my attention right now.

Keep It Flowing

If only such decisions came nicely in sequence — but they don't. There are games that seem so crowded, there's something you could call all the time. The referee has to juggle the decisions and decide what's most important. It's a fast game, and one way to avoid trouble is to let it flow. The referee is busy, so are the players, and it's his job to keep it that way. When the players are concentrating on playing, they don't have time to complain or to say or do nasty things to each other. The referee keeps up the pace by blowing the whistle sparingly if he can, but firmly if he has to,

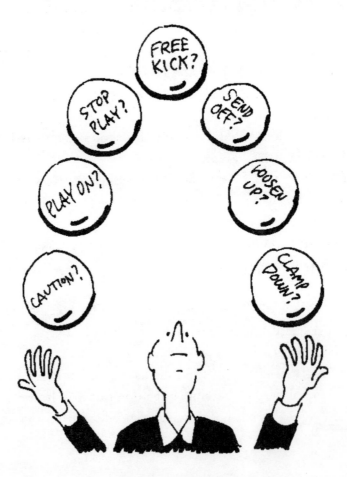

indicating the approximate spot, giving a quick "play" signal and running backwards downfield for good positioning while his eyes are on the play. That way, if a player wants to dissent, the ref isn't even there! "Don't just stand there, do something" is a good rule to follow. Of course, close to the penalty area the referee is more concerned about correct placement and the defenders' distance from the free kick, and he is always alert for any shenanigans behind his back while he is so occupied. The more constantly the ball is in play, the less chance of trouble. Nothing is more destructive than a chopped-up game full of stoppages and delays. Some referees like to blow that whistle too much. The players and fans won't like it and they will start to concentrate more on the refereeing than on the game itself. And that is really bad . . . not only for the referee but for the game.

Levels of Play

This balancing act by the referee also depends on the level of the competition. In a game with older, experienced players, he should let them play as much as possible, but on the other hand there may be more fouls. If players seem tense at the beginning, the referee may call things close to let the players know that he's in charge, and to allow them to "read" him. However, if he senses that players are relatively relaxed and are concentrating on their own business rather than his, he should relax also and let them play. He can always clamp down later if necessary. Many games have deteriorated because the referee handed out yellow cards too early when it was not strictly necessary. That might irritate players to the point where they begin to foul even more, and now the referee has no choice but to shift to giving out red cards. However, a well-timed yellow card can do wonders and help settle down a game that is threatening to get out of hand. Making these decisions correctly separates the best referees from the pack.

The question is always how to honor the three principles of safety, fairness, and enjoyment. At lower levels of competition, the referee's role may become that of an educator. Inexperienced players must learn partly from him — not by what he tells them but by the calls he makes — what is a proper throw-in, what is dangerous play or obstruction, a legal versus an illegal charge, or what the laws mean by "intentional." At this level also, the referee must strike a balance between stopping play for infractions and maintaining the flow of the game and letting these players have a good experience. Achieving that precarious balance has over the years been my most difficult task and my most rewarding experience.

Don't call what you see — Call what you must!

3

The Laws and the Spirit

THE *LAWS OF THE GAME,* SHORT AS THEY ARE COMPARED with the rule books of other sports, are the basic laws of soccer, in the light of which the numerous specific decisions are made. In the hundred and fifteen years or so of the game's existence, these laws have changed very little, but the "Decisions of the International F(ootball) A(ssociation) Board" spell out how the laws are to be applied. For example, the "Decisions" attached to Law XIV, which deals with the penalty kick, are twice as long as the text of the law itself. Even so, as we saw

in Chapter 2, "Reading the Game," the referee's decisions are never automatic. Rather, they are influenced by such variables as the level of play
and the experience and disposition of the players. Some people may find
that confusing. If referees do not adhere strictly to the *Laws of the Game*,
how are we to achieve worldwide consistency in their application? Most
of us witnessed some inconsistent applications of the offside law during
the World Cup 1994 that confused players and led to some unfortunate
results. That did not happen because the laws are inadequate but because
some of the laws are not applied the same way on all continents.

The Spirit of the Law

No matter how detailed the "Decisions" attached to each Law may become, they cannot include every instance that may occur in a given game.
The best we can hope for is that referees do not only know the letter of
the laws but that they understand the intent or *spirit* of each law and
have the wisdom to translate that into fair decisions. That is a daunting
challenge to every man or woman in the black uniform. A good referee
never makes a call mindlessly, simply "because the rule book says so." The
rule book itself gives a wonderful example of this when in Law V it
establishes the advantage clause. It says that the referee "shall refrain from
penalizing in cases where he is satisfied that, by doing so, he would be
giving an advantage to the offending team." It says in effect: Hey, don't
interfere with the game just because there was a foul. We are looking for
justice, not punishment!

Three Illustrations of the Spirit of the Law

1. Law XII defines violations that are penalized by an indirect free kick
such as dangerous play, fair charges away from the ball, intentional obstruction, and delaying tactics by the goalkeeper. It also lists charging the
goalkeeper as a violation, except when he:

(a) is holding the ball;

(b) is obstructing an opponent;

(c) has passed outside his goal area.

As you know, the modern goalkeeper more often than not takes possession of the ball outside the goal area. You also know what would probably happen if a referee applied exception (a) literally: there's a legal shoulder charge against a goalkeeper who has just caught the ball — the ball is jostled loose — a defender shoves the opponent in order to protect his goalkeeper — that, in turn, calls for retaliation — and here is the likely result: a penalty kick and cautions or ejections. Fortunately, we don't have to worry. Provision (a) has not been changed, but the "Decisions" appended to Law XII forbid "intentionally obstruct[ing] the opposing goalkeeper" when he is trying to clear the ball. That should be enough to avoid such messy situations. At the last several World Cups as well as before the Olympic Games at Barcelona in 1992, referees were specifically instructed not to allow any interference with the goalkeeper. The spirit of the game tells us clearly that in today's game the goalkeeper is an endangered species and that he is to be protected at all times, unless he is playing the ball with his feet like any other player.

2. Law XII also includes the "four step" rule after the goalkeeper has gained possession. Does that mean that the referee stands there watching like a hawk to count every step of the goalkeeper between his gaining possession and throwing or kicking the ball away? Of course not. The four-step rule was instituted in order to keep the goalkeeper from roaming freely in the penalty area while holding the ball as a delaying tactic. Applying the *spirit* of the law here means asking yourself: is the goalkeeper getting rid of the ball reasonably quickly? Say he takes two steps after making a save, catches his breath, looks upfield, and takes three or four more steps before releasing the ball. That takes only four or five seconds. The spirit of the law has been satisfied. Soccer referees are not asked to be miserly bookkeepers or cops! You agree, I'm sure, that a good police officer does not ticket people who stop their cars two inches over the line at a traffic light. It's the spirit of the law that counts, not the letter. Referees are there to facilitate the proper playing of the game, not to catch players in violations.

3. Law XIV deals with the taking of a penalty kick. The law has two

provisions that can ruin the game if the referee takes the law too literally. The first provision is that players from both teams, except the goalkeeper and the kicker, shall be outside the penalty area and the ten-yard arc, and behind the ball, until the kick has been taken. A player of either side who enters the penalty box before the kick has been taken is guilty of *encroachment*, i.e. of unfairly interfering with the proper taking of the kick or defending against it. Thus, technically, if an attacking player steps into the box just before the ball is kicked and the ball goes into the net, the kick should be retaken — so says the law! Similarly, if a defensive player steps into the box early and the kick does not score, the law again stipulates a retake. Just visualize this happening and the referee following the letter of the law! Doesn't a retake seem to be unnecessarily harsh in most cases of minor encroachment? Fortunately, in practice this law is never applied, *except when the encroachment did in fact directly interfere* with the kicker or the goalkeeper. Let us look at this situation more closely.

In the first instance we mentioned, when an attacking player encroaches, let us assume that the kicker placed the ball beautifully in a corner and the goalkeeper had no chance, nor was he hindered by the encroachment. Would justice be served if the referee nullified the goal and ordered a re-kick? In the second instance, with a defensive player encroaching, and assuming that the kicker was not disadvantaged, while the goalkeeper made a marvelous save: Would it be fair to give the kicker another chance just because of a technicality? Would the *spirit of the law* be satisfied? Of course not. Only if there is both intent and actual interference, is the retake (and probably a yellow card) appropriate. Clearly the spirit of the law would be violated if the referee ordered a retake for a minor technical infraction, and the players would be properly upset!

But, someone will ask, what if the goalkeeper were to parry the ball, and the kicker's teammate, who had crossed the line too early, got hold of it and scored? No problem there: now the attacking player has taken advantage of his encroachment, and since the penalty kick did not score, the referee should, according to paragraph 4 (c) of the F.A. Board "Decisions" award an indirect free kick to the defense. In the case of a defender who has encroached and kicks the ball away after the goalkeeper parries it, a retake is in order since the encroaching player did take an unfair advantage. Some people think that an indirect free kick for the offense would be more fair here also, but the law properly stipulates a retake in this case. Generally there is no problem as long as we observe the basic spirit of the rule: was the attacking side unfairly prevented from scoring a goal, or the defense from saving one? This case illustrates a general principle of refereeing: Never give anyone an unfair advantage just because of a technical infraction! Experienced referees let common sense rule.

The danger of this chapter is that it seems to give the referee room to be "creative" according to his instincts and to do what — to him — seems fair. Some instructors may think that this is not a proper subject for, say, an entry-level clinic. But if our young aspiring colleagues work a lot of games, they will soon encounter the question of the law's letter and its spirit. They may also encounter it as players or see it on television. So we must talk in all honesty about what one might call "the finer points of the game." The sooner one learns them, the better.

The law lives not in the letter but in the spirit!

4

Game Situations I

Advantage ♦ *Offside* ♦ *Scoring* ♦ *Intent*
♦ *Stopping Play* ♦ *Cautions and Ejections*
♦ *Reversing Decisions* ♦ *Drop Balls* ♦
Injuries ♦ *Interference* ♦ *Keeping Time*
♦ *Delaying Tactics* ♦ *Overtime* ♦
After the Game

N OW LET US LOOK AT OTHER GAME SITUATIONS AND see *how* both the letter and the spirit of the laws should be applied. The subtopics for this chapter refer primarily to general rules and situations, whereas the next chapter, "Game Situations II," deals primarily with Laws XII through XIV: fouls, misconduct, and free kicks, including the penalty kick.

Compared to the rule books of other sports such as American football and basketball, the *Laws of the Game* of soccer are brief, and even the "Decisions of the F.A. Board" do not go into all possible details. They mention only one instance of "dangerous play," for example, and never define in detail what kinds of conduct are "ungentlemanly." That is largely up to referees to decide though, in the course of time, broad general agreement has been reached about such concepts. Then there are the simple-but-difficult advantage clause and the technicalities of restarts that can involve subtleties of which many players, spectators, and beginning referees are not aware. These concrete game situations, however, make up the nitty-gritty part of refereeing. They also form the basis for the lively arguments we may have at referees' clinics over what one should do in the many situations that can and do occur. Only one thing is sure:

No two situations are exactly alike.

As we saw in Chapter 2, every playing situation is a composite of the teams' skills and dispositions on a given day, or of the weather and other variables that can affect a particular game. Referees must anticipate some of these factors as part of their pre-game mental preparation. They must also be ready to adjust to them during the game, for even then those conditions can change.

ADVANTAGE CLAUSE

Law V (b) stipulates that the referee shall "refrain from penalizing in cases where he is satisfied that, by doing so, he would be giving an advantage to the offending team." What is and what is not a meaningful advantage for a team that warrants giving the "play on" signal instead of awarding a free kick? If you are the referee, you have to make a split-second decision. Is the attacking team on a fast break with a good scoring chance? Do they have the wind in their backs? In youth play, a team may get more advantage from a free kick if they have a player with a strong leg. There may be a clear advantage for the defense when they are fouled but gain the ball and can immediately start a counter attack. But you should probably blow the whistle for an offensive foul when the defense gains possession under pressure deep in its own zone and tries to clear the ball. What if there is a rather serious defensive foul but a clear scoring chance for the offense? You should let play go on and caution or eject the offending player at the next dead ball.

A very important change in the advantage clause was announced by FIFA in June 1996. That addition allows the referee to blow the whistle for the original foul if the "advantage" he signaled previously does not materialize within a few seconds after his "play on" signal. Now the referee is no longer on the hot seat, since he can undo his initial advantage call. On the other hand, if the advantage *does* materialize into a scoring chance or goal, the referee can still congratulate himself. The Board did not intend to be generous to the referee, of course. They must have thought that this change would increase the use of the advantage call and thereby decrease the number of play interruptions.

At this early date there is no telling how the new rule will be applied. It is clear that the F.A. Board does not intend anything like the delayed foul call used in hockey, where the foul is not called until the fouled team loses possession. Typically, the play will be called back if the original foul is followed almost immediately by a team's loss of the ball to their opponent.

OFFSIDE

Both Law XI and the diagrams depicting basic offside situations in our rule books are adequate for most situations. Still, a few illustrations of an attacking player "interfering" or "gaining an advantage" may be helpful.

1. An attacker is coming back from an offside position: is he just returning to an onside position without any attempt to participate in the play, or does he make a move toward a ball coming his way and thus try to take advantage of his position? In the latter case, he should of course be called offside.

2. With one or more attacking players in an offside position, a forward pass may be intercepted for a routine save by the goalkeeper. He can then throw or punt it into play perhaps more effectively than if you awarded the indirect free kick for offside. In situations farther from the goal, however, the defenders may let their guard down because they expect the offside call, while an attacking player who was onside quickly takes advantage of the situation. This happened during the Brazil-Netherlands

game in World Cup 1994. On a Brazilian forward pass, the Dutch defenders appealed because of Brazilian forward Romario's offside position. Romario made no attempt at playing the ball, but his teammate Bebeto rushed in from his onside position on the wing, took the ball, and scored. Obviously, these Dutch professionals were used to a different practice in Europe. In this respect, it seems, the international game is in a transition phase. In some countries, players are still routinely called offside, even though they are not taking advantage of their offside position. In recent years, however, FIFA is directing referees not to take away legitimate scoring chances from the attacking team. The Bebeto case is a good example of that practice. Meanwhile, consistency in the application of the offside law remains a problem.

3. There is frequently a melee of several players close to the goal, where the quick movements of players on both teams can easily place an attacking player momentarily in an offside situation just as his fellow player shoots on goal. That player is not "taking advantage." That changes, of course, if the ball bounces back to him off the goalpost or the keeper. Now he must be called offside.

4. A player dribbles past the defenders with the ball, while a fellow player is running a few paces ahead of him and slightly to the side in an offside position: Is the player without the ball perhaps distracting the goalkeeper and thus interfering? In this case, you should trust the goalkeeper to concentrate on the player with the ball. What if that player fakes a pass to the player to his left, causing the goalkeeper to react, and then beats the goalkeeper on the other side? This is tricky, since the player in offside position is not *directly* doing anything to influence play, yet his presence is a distinct factor. Go ahead, discuss this situation in your meetings! Perhaps you will think of other possible scenarios.

5. A player is in an offside position as his fellow player takes a shot on goal from farther out. How close can the offside player be to the keeper before he is interfering? And how do you as a referee or linesman distinguish between a pass and a shot on goal? What's the distinction — intent? Basically, you should judge only whether or not the offside player *is* close enough and *does* interfere. Don't be too hasty in making that decision. Of course, if the shot or pass is parried by the keeper (the same as if it bounced off the goal post), and is now played by the offside player, he should be called. A referee or linesman does not judge the player's intent, but rather what he sees happening. The Law does not ask you to be a mind reader but only a judge of the facts.

6. An attacking player takes himself out of the play by kneeling down or briefly stepping out of bounds to indicate that he is not participating in the play. This common practice should be recognized as legal but no longer

necessary with the new emphasis on a player's taking advantage of his offside position. But a defensive player stepping out of bounds in order to "create" an offside situation for the attackers: that's a no-no! In fact, it is ungentlemanly conduct.

7. Good cooperation between referee and linesmen is crucial, and therefore pre-game instructions are important. In most cases, the referee may assume that the linesmen know what is meant by "interference" or "taking advantage." Linesmen should judge the situation and raise the flag (raise it and not wave it!) only if, in their judgment, there is clear danger of an illegal score. Referees and linesmen should have good eye contact. The dangerous situation may resolve itself within a second and cause the referee to wave the linesman off. However: he should use caution. What is, for example, a routine ball for the adult goalkeeper may not be so for a twelve-year-old. It's better to be sure than to be sorry.

SCORING

Law X, "Method of Scoring," is the shortest of the *Laws of the Game*, probably because it is so simple: a goal is scored when the ball crosses completely over the goal line between the goalposts unless it is intentionally propelled by an attacker's hand or arm, or is scored directly from a throw-in, a goal kick, or the kickoff. In addition, the F.A. Board has ruled that a goal cannot be scored *directly from a free kick* by a team into its own goal, either from inside or outside the penalty area. We know that if a goal kick or other free kick is awarded to the defense in its own penalty area, the ball must be kicked beyond the penalty area before any other player may play it. Therefore, if the ball is kicked into its own goal by the defense, the referee should simply order a *retake*, even if it touched the goalie. Should a free kick by the defense from outside the penalty area go into the goal *directly*, i.e. without being touched by another player (that

includes the goalkeeper), the referee should award a corner kick to the opponents.

Net checks by the linesmen just before the beginning of play are important. In addition to leaving no holes at the posts or top bar, the net should not be strung so tightly at the upper corners that a ball could bounce back outside the goal after having passed the goal line. That happened twice in my career, once in a tournament final, and it created considerable confusion.

If a game is played without nets, the referee should not allow a goal before checking unobtrusively with the linesman. In fact, that is something he should always do.

INTENT OR DELIBERATION

As of 1996, Law XII no longer talks of fouls that are committed "intentionally." Instead, it speaks of offenses committed "in a manner considered by the referee to be careless, reckless, or involving disproportionate force." Many of us will still, I think, sometimes find the concepts of intent of deliberation useful. To be sure, a player's slap at the ball with his hand may simply be a reflex action, especially when the ball bounces up to his chest. We may now call that "careless," rather than "intentional." The idea is still the same, however: it's a matter of whether he played the ball or the ball played him. Similarly, a charge with "cleats showing" may be considered reckless rather than something done with malice afore-thought. As we have seen before, referees are not asked to read the players' minds. Rather, they judge what the players did. That explains why FIFA has deleted most references to intent.

In other places the laws clearly recognize that we must sometimes detect not only the recklessness or violence involved but also the kind of deliberation that calls for a yellow or red card. A foul committed in re-taliation differs from a foul that is due to inexperience or overenthusiasm. F.A. Board "Decisions" (13) for Law XII specifies that a player who "im-pedes" an opponent with "an obvious opportunity to score a goal" should be sent off for serious foul play. Paragraph (14) applies the same penalty to the goalkeeper who intentionally handles the ball outside the penalty area to deny an opponent a scoring opportunity.

Experienced players know very well what they are doing, so in their case few infractions are inadvertent and they must be dealt with sternly. At the same time, young players must also be penalized for uncontrolled play. They will not learn what is allowed and what is not unless they are taught by the referee's calls.

STOPPING PLAY

Play can be stopped only by the referee's whistle. Since players sometimes anticipate a call and stop playing or even pick up the ball before there is a whistle, we sometimes admonish them to "play the whistle." In a differ-ent sense I sometimes want to tell a referee to "play the whistle" rather than just blowing it. A referee should "speak" with his whistle and communicate to the players what he is calling and how he feels about it. This is my own repertoire on the whistle:

♦   a short tweet for routine infractions (and for routine out-of-bounds only if necessary);

♦   a quick toot-toot-toot to catch a player's intention when the ball is already dead but needs to be moved into position, or to make a player wait a moment for some other correction;

♦   one good strong whistle for an injury, a definite foul, or a corner kick or penalty kick;

♦   several strong blasts in the case of players fighting or threatening hostilities.

The way a referee blows his whistle signals to players that he's in command and distinguishes between minor and major infractions.

CAUTIONS AND EJECTIONS

Another form of communication that requires a sense of proportion is carding a player. There is something dramatic about the situation, and you as well as the guilty player are on center stage. You will have to learn how or when to use the card most effectively. Don't give it for the wrong reasons, e.g. just because you are mad or feel insecure. First, there are certain mandatory cautions and ejections defined in the *Laws*. Still, use your judgment in deciding the spirit as well as the letter of the Law. In all other instances use your discretion. Basically you give a card only because in your judgment the game needs it, not because the player dissented from your call and you are going to show him who's boss.

The time of the game can be important. If you start handing out cards too early, pretty soon you have no more options left and may have to go to red cards sooner than desirable, so use them sparingly. If the players don't respect you, no cards will change their minds. You have to earn their respect by your objectivity and demeanor. On the other hand, don't hesitate to use the cards. When they were instituted in the seventies, they gave the referee an icon, a visible signal of his role in maintaining discipline. I believe they have worked the way they were intended to.

There's a *when* but also a *how*. Sometimes I find myself not taking enough time to caution properly. Yes, I want to get on with the game, but I should not just vaguely wave the card at the player's back. Neither should I run after him or call him with my finger pointing to my feet as if I were calling my dog. If he walks away, I call out his number without shouting, have him face me and tell him I can't let his behavior pass. Whatever technique you use, give proper weight to the occasion. Don't lecture the player. Write down the time, the violation, and the player's name and number. The calmer you are, the more credibility you have. It was not you who caused the stoppage — it was the player! Taking your time is part of game control. It sinks in with the other players.

REVERSING DECISIONS

Sooner or later, every referee will have to deal with the awkward situation of having made an unfortunate decision he wishes to undo. He or his linesman, for example, may, shortly after intermission, when the teams have changed ends, point for a throw-in in the wrong direction. Like some other mistakes, this one is easily reversible, as long as the mistake is realized before the throw-in is taken. Usually, the players will let you know immediately, and you will change your signal. Be sure, however, that you give players on either side who had changed positions because of the mistaken signal time to recover their position. If you don't, the other team may take quick advantage and launch a fast break that could result in an unfortunate goal.

Foul calls, too, are reversible if the referee realizes he pointed in the wrong direction. Even an apparent goal may be annulled if the linesman brings to the referee's attention that one of the attackers committed, say, a hands foul just before the score, or that the goalkeeper was interfered with. Such a ticklish situation can be avoided if the referee makes it a habit *never* to award a goal before he has checked his linesman's signal. As long as the game has not been restarted, most decisions are reversible.

Some erroneous calls are particularly awkward and do not allow of a simple or elegant solution. If, for example, the linesman flags an offside and then realizes that he had overlooked a defender who was on the goal line with his keeper, what would you do? If you whistled for the offside, play has stopped. How will you restart? The technically correct way is to have a drop ball. Where? Supposedly at the spot where the receiving player was mistakenly called offside. How close to the goal might that be? Just recently, I saw a goal scored almost immediately from such a ball dropped by the referee just outside the goal box. That's why some referees insist that a wrong offside call, however unfortunate, is not reversible. My own choice in this stressful situation is to take the drop ball as far away from the goal as I possibly can. Another technique is to walk over to a random couple of players not too close to the goal and drop the ball while saying, "OK, guys, wait until it bounces." That usually helps to avert the danger of an immediate score. You don't have to make a big ceremony out of every drop ball. Let the spirit guide you!

An inadvertent whistle — which one of us has not been guilty of it? That's why I would discourage referees from running with the whistle in their mouth like a basketball referee. If it happens, however, restart with a drop ball. Do not, having made a mistake, make it worse by quickly shouting, "Play on, my fault!" That will only create more confusion.

The same principle applies to other supposed mistakes. If you have awarded a possibly questionable penalty kick to one team, never try to restore the balance by later awarding a questionable penalty kick to the other team. If you do, you will have both sides mad at you instead of one.

One measure of your ability as a referee will be your aptness in acknowledging your mistake and choosing the correct and fairest restart.

DROP BALLS

I have not seen a drop ball in an international game for quite a while. Inexperienced or fainthearted referees, on the other hand, tend to rely on drop balls to let them off the hook. When in doubt, that's their safety net. They tend to call "simultaneous fouls" and drop the ball rather than giving a free kick. If they call an out-of-bounds differently from the linesman: drop ball. Generally, that use of the drop ball is to the players a sign of the referee's insecurity. So use the drop ball sparingly.

The most common use of the drop ball comes in the case of an injury. Even then, however, you can usually afford to wait until the ball is kicked out of bounds or the injured player's team gains possession. If the injury appears serious enough to stop play instantly, at the restart you may follow the international practice of dropping the ball in front of a player whose team lost possession when you whistled the ball dead. This gesture may be misunderstood by American teams and audiences. Perhaps referees can take the lead in educating them in this form of soccer etiquette. Similarly, players should be encouraged to throw in the ball to an opponent who has politely kicked the ball out of bounds in a similar situation. It is a nice gesture that helps to maintain a good atmosphere in the game.

Other Restarts

When the referee blows the whistle for any rules infraction, play is considered to be stopped at that moment, even if some players do not hear the whistle and continue playing. When that happens, the referee should insist on the stoppage of play. He should not allow play to continue because the infraction was minor. If the infraction wasn't serious enough to bother, why did he blow the whistle in the first place? Here too, not enforcing your first whistle will only create confusion and you may lose the players' respect. What if a foul or some form of misconduct occurs after the whistle? The referee must deal with that separately with a warning, a caution, or a disqualification. The restart should be based on the first whistle with either an indirect or a direct kick. Where? There is often some confusion on that point.

Generally, direct or indirect free kicks given for infractions on the field of play *and with the ball in play* are taken at the place where the foul or misconduct occurred. For example, if the defense commits a foul inside the penalty box, though the ball has long since been cleared upfield, the ball must be brought back for the appropriate penalty. Also, when a recognized player who was off the field for an injury returns without the referee's permission, the penalty will be a caution and an indirect free kick at the place of the infraction.

For misconduct that takes place off the field, such as fights between players or dissent from the bench, the referee will issue a yellow or red card and restart the game with a drop ball at the place where the ball was when he stopped play. The same applies if play is stopped for an injury, unless the injury was the result of a foul, in which case you will have awarded a free kick. Like free kicks, a drop ball should never be executed closer to the goal line than the six-yard-line.

INJURIES

When a player goes down, the referee will often find himself caught between a rock and hard place. If he blows the whistle immediately to stop play, he may be criticized for unnecessary interference with play, especially if that player's team is in possession of the ball and launching an attack. If he allows play to go on, he may be accused of not caring and risking a player's health — especially if the player's team is on defense, of course. The referee should be aware of that difference. Most injuries are insignificant, and the player who went down is usually remarkably quick to recover when the ball is in his vicinity. Unless there was a serious foul that caused the player to go down, the referee should keep one eye on the player and allow play to go on as long as his team has possession or until there is a natural stoppage of play *and he does not deem the player to be seriously injured.* If possible, he should be careful not to disadvantage the team on offense, because a defensive player may be faking an injury and stay down longer than necessary. If the referee does stop play while the ball is live, the eventual restart should be a drop ball at the place where the ball was at that moment.*

If the injury requires treatment, and only then, the referee should signal for a trainer to come on to the field. He should record the stoppage of play, both to keep proper track of time lapsed and for his game report. The referee should never risk possible litigation by trying to treat the injured player himself. Especially if there is an open wound, he should

---

* Present High School Federation rules specify that an indirect free kick should be awarded to the team in possession at the time of the whistle. If no team had clear possession, play should be resumed with a drop ball.

stay close only to discourage other players from getting involved. If it turns out that the injury is serious enough to require professional treatment by a physician or an emergency medical technician (EMT), a com-

plete and careful game report should include the player's name and team. The referee would do well to express his concern after the game and to ask where he might call to find out about the player's condition — but only, I would recommend,  if the cause of the injury is not controversial. This is both a natural gesture of caring and a proper way to lessen the probability of official inquiries or litigation.

INTERFERENCE

The problem of an animal or another "outside agent" interfering with the ball before it enters the goal is also solved with a drop ball, no matter how unfair that may seem to one side or the other. If the outside agent is a spectator trying to prevent a goal but not making contact, and the ball enters the goal, the score shall count ("Decisions," Law X). If contact is made, restart with a drop ball after dealing with the obvious conduct problem. The referee himself, however clumsy he may be, is never counted as an outside agent. Rather, the Law simply makes him a part of the playing field, which would seem to put him in his proper place.

KEEPING TIME

Again we have to cope with different competitions, age groups, and rule books. Above all, make sure that coaches and players know how long the halves last and under what overtime rules (if any) you are playing. If the rules don't specify, but the teams insist on playing overtime, let them, but don't participate. Your job is done.

Always use two watches, a running-time watch and a stopwatch. At the beginning of each half, write down the actual time. That will bail you out if you should forget to restart your stop watch after a time-out. Play it safe!

If time is kept by an official timekeeper off the field, that's easy, except when there is a last-second shot on goal. There was one just recently in a Division III play-off game. If the ball is not over the goal line when the buzzer goes, it's no goal.

What if you are keeping the official time on the field? You may have noticed that in professional games time never seems to expire while the ball is dead or when it's being played in a tight situation close to one of the goals. As you must know, that is pure coincidence. When regulation time is up, the referee should decide for himself how long he is going to play "referee's time" plus whatever other time he may have to add for unforeseen delays. Stick to that decision without telling anyone how much time you are adding. If there is a stadium clock, let it be stopped at the end of regulation time unless the league has special rules. During the game I may answer players who ask how much time is left, but not in the final stages, except in a general way, "We're in the last few minutes." To be more specific invites second guessing by players.

DELAYING TACTICS

We all know the situation: one team is a goal ahead with fifteen minutes to go, and the opposition is gathering steam. Now the defense may kick the ball upfield as far as they can, hoping they can stop the next attack. OK. So can they help it if the ball goes fifteen rows into the stands and it takes twenty seconds to retrieve it? You bet they can! Then there is the player who suddenly has an "equipment breakdown" or a cramp. Some are very good actors. Or a spectator suddenly loses control of his dog. You know what to do: Just let the teams know you are adding time.

In the high school or college game you may have a problem. Or two: if time is kept by a timekeeper on the sideline, and if the winning coach craftily substitutes several players every time the ball goes out of bounds. Keep things fair. Tell the coach and the players that you're stopping the clock, and tell the timekeeper to watch for your "time out" signals. If there is no official timekeeper, just use your own discretion.

OVERTIME

Be sure before the game, especially during play-off time or in tournaments, what your competition's rules are in case of a tie. Discuss them briefly with coaches and captains. When overtime is to be played, everyone should know how long the periods are and how much time is allowed between periods.

If after the stipulated overtime the game is to be decided by penalty kicks, be sure what the mechanics are. There are slight differences between FIFA rules and High School rules. Go over the mechanics with your linesmen during the break, and then with team captains. They should know, for example, which players are eligible to participate, and whether or when they can substitute goalkeepers. An ounce of prevention here can save you a ton of trouble.

AFTER THE GAME

Perhaps Yogi Berra had it right when he said, "The game ain't over until it's over," but in soccer it's not over until you blow the final whistle and you gather up your linesmen and leave the field together. It's nice if there is a dressing room where you can unwind and chat with your linesmen, but that's the exception rather than the rule. In any case, don't hang around to allow coaches, players, spectators, or the media to engage you in "post-game interviews." Don't accept an invitation for a beer in the club house. Some referees seem to enjoy standing around to accept congratulations (from the winning team, of course). Don't! Your only job is to see to it that everybody leaves healthy and happy. Go home, stretch out your legs and congratulate yourself on the great game you had. Or lie awake at night over the one play you messed up. You asked for it. And you'll be out there again tomorrow or next week, we hope.

REF DREAMS

5

Game Situations II

Fouls and Misconduct ♦
Throw-ins ♦ *Obstruction*
♦ *Intentional Hands* ♦
Taking Free Kicks ♦ *The Penalty Kick*

FOULS AND MISCONDUCT

Direct and Indirect Kicks

You know which ten infractions require *direct free kicks*. Just refresh your memory from time to time by going over Law XII and Law XIII. Illegal charges are:

◆ three with the legs (kicking, tripping, jumping);

◆ two with the body (charging violently or/and from behind);

◆ four with the hands (striking, pushing, holding — and handling the ball intentionally);

◆ plus the most recent addition of spitting at a player (which is considered violent conduct, penalized with an ejection).

These are all very clear, at least on paper.

All other infractions *while the ball is in play*, such as offside, danger-ous play, obstruction, and ungentlemanly conduct, require *indirect free kicks.* The referee's signal for an indirect kick should be clear (one arm raised), and inexperienced players would benefit also from being told: "Indirect." Just remember that you must never give a free kick for anything that happens when the ball is dead.

Misconduct

You can, of course, penalize players for infractions that occur after the whistle. That includes half-time and even the time you spend on the field before the kickoff. Some of these are for violent conduct (fighting, kicking, striking, spitting, etc.), requiring red cards, but many will be for vari-ous kinds of ungentlemanly conduct such as dissent, taunting, kicking the ball away after a whistle, feigning injury, and other forms of gamesmanship that can spoil a good game.

Again, when these things happen while the ball is dead, they cannot be penalized by awarding free kicks. Rather, they will require cautions or ejections. The restart is based on the situation for which play was stopped originally, no matter how serious was the foul. (See Chapter 4 for *Restarts*)

Live Ball Fouls

It is impossible to sketch here the many permutations that may occur between a ball in play and two or more players intent upon gaining possession of it. Competitive soccer allows quite a bit of physical contact, and the referee's job is to keep it in bounds. Quite often the distinction between a contact foul and dangerous play will not be clear. For example, there are two common situations that are often misjudged.

HIGH BALLS

During the flight of the ball from a punt, a goal kick, or a corner kick, the referee should be watching the players who are moving in to play it while they themselves and others watch the ball in flight. This is the moment for the quick little push in the back that throws an opponent off balance, and for obstruction and holding. Other common fouls in that situation are going up over the opponent to head the ball, or going under a player who has jumped to head the ball. Direct or indirect kick? It depends on the kind of foul and the severity. Also the player who turns his body as he jumps toward the ball and slams into his opponent should be called. He is not controlling his body.

SLIDING TACKLES

Sliding tackles seem to be favored by young players who have played baseball. In soccer, however, one is not sliding at full speed toward second base but toward the ball at the feet of an opponent. Once the sliding player is into his motion, he cannot change directions, yet a player must always control his body. The proper way is usually to come in from the side and kick the ball away from in front of the opponent, who then may fall over the leg of the tackler. A head-on sliding tackle almost always results in dangerous play. Similarly, the sliding tackle from behind is usually an illegal charge because only very skilled players can execute it cleanly. Tackling with a foot up, showing cleats, is definitely dangerous. It can easily result in an injury to the opponent and warrants a yellow card to the tackler.

PLAYING THE PLAYER

Dangerous Play

Everybody knows about it, but few players and spectators know how it is applied. "High kick, ref!" — but was it dangerous? Dangerous to whom, to a stationary or to an incoming player? Watch the timing when two players attempt to play an incoming ball: who was first into his motion, the player with the foot extended to play the ball, or his opponent trying to head it away? The player who was last is the one who causes the dangerous play even if he is injured in the process. There is no such foul as "high kicking." The player's foot is perhaps not higher than his knee. The question is whether he commits dangerous play.

Other Examples

♦   A player holding the ball between his legs while sitting or lying on the ground. It can be considered dangerous play because as opponents try to kick the ball in his possession, he is endangering himself. This, despite the strange wording of the F.A. Board's "Decisions," Law XII (7), which says that the player is legally obstructing and may be charged by an opponent. That could lead to mayhem. If a player covers the ball without playing it, he could also be penalized for game delay.

♦   A player who kicks wildly into the melee of a loose ball and other players' feet.

♦   A player running into the keeper because the keeper dropped the ball, or diving on top of him in the resulting scramble, even if he is trying to play the loose ball. Since this is an offensive foul in front of the goal, it makes no difference whether you call it dangerous play or charging.

♦   A player who kicks at a ball at his opponent's feet as hard as he can, without regard for that player's or his own safety. This is not uncommon in youth soccer and may sometimes qualify as violent play. Yes, I hear them: "He played the ball, ref!" But playing the ball cannot include simultaneously slamming into the opponent's body or kicking his shin on the follow-through. We have to educate players about this. Soccer is not like playing tiddly winks, but it's not war either!

♦   The spectacular bicycle kick that spectators love can be flawless or it can be dangerous play depending on the position of the other players. In the face of an oncoming player it can be dangerous play. On the other hand, the kicker is not responsible for players behind him whom he cannot see and who are usually only in danger of being hit by the ball rather than his foot. I have seen too many beautiful goals nullified for alleged dangerous play.

THROW-INS

Although studies have shown that in the majority of cases the team taking the throw-in loses the ball very quickly, throw-ins must not be taken lightly. A powerful throw deep into the penalty area, including the acrobatic somersault-throw that we often see in high-school games, can create immediate scoring chances. The important thing for referee and linesmen is to avoid any conflicts or confusion about ruling which team gets to throw the ball and whether a throw is legal.

It is customary to have the linesmen judge the position of the thrower's feet (behind or on the line), and the referee takes the hands. The ball must be thrown, not just dropped, and the thrower should face the direction in which he is throwing the ball. My practice is to instruct the linesmen to flag the out-of-bounds for the entire sideline or goal line. He should indicate the direction of the throw (or goal kick vs. corner) only for his own half of the sideline or his side of the goal line and leave the rest to the referee, unless the referee asks him to indicate direction with a hand signal. That is, considering their most likely positions, a reasonable division of labor and avoids the awkwardness of conflicting signals.

The rules permit a player taking the throw-in to bounce the ball off an opposing player as long as it is not violent, but I advise strongly against it. We should avoid the confrontations to which it might easily lead. Similarly, a player standing close enough to the thrower to be a hindrance is being provocative in a way similar to a player who intentionally takes up a position in front of the goalkeeper who has just caught the ball. Such practices are rightly considered "bush-league," and the player should be warned.

OBSTRUCTION — LEGAL AND ILLEGAL

Legal obstruction is screening an opponent from the ball in one's possession, i.e. in immediate playing distance. That is common knowledge. Some

LEGAL OBSTRUCTION

referees and players do not know that a player who screens the ball may be charged from behind, though not violently or with the hands.

Illegal obstruction is preventing an opponent with one's body from reaching a free ball or keeping him from tackling one's own teammate — often the keeper — who is in possession of the ball. Particular forms of illegal obstruction are:

♦   setting a "pick" for a fellow player;

♦   slowing down or dodging right and left to keep an opponent from reaching the ball before it goes out of bounds, unless one stays within immediate striking distance of the ball;

♦   crossing the line between one's own goalkeeper and an oncoming opponent without playing the ball (though this seems to have become a routine play by defenders all over the world);

♦   jumping in front of a player who has just played the ball forward,

ILLEGAL OBSTRUCTION

and preventing him from going after it.

Illegal obstruction is penalized by an indirect free kick. It is therefore not thought of as a serious foul. Yet it has the same basic effect as more physical fouls because it separates a player illegally from the ball. It can be particularly irritating if the ball rolls harmlessly out of bounds and a free throw or a corner kick is awarded to obstructing player's team. The referee should recognize illegal obstruction and not shrug it off.

INTENTIONAL HANDS

In the previous chapter we discussed "intent" in a general way. Many of us saw the illegal goal scored in World Cup 1986 by the Argentinian star Maradona, who used his fist instead of his head to punch the ball into England's goal. The referee missed it and, apparently, so did the linesman. In a later interview, Maradona said: "Half of it was the hand of God, the other half was mine."

I would call a hand foul such as Maradona's deliberate, and not only disallow the goal but also caution the player for misconduct. This is, after all, very much like the F.A. Board's decision in the obverse case when a player "denies his opponents a goal, or an obvious goal-scoring opportunity, by intentionally handling the ball . . . ." It instructs the referee to send the player off

INTENTIONAL HANDLING

for "serious foul play." The flagrant score with the hand almost falls in that category and should earn the player a yellow card.

The basic criterion for judging a hands violation is whether the ball strikes the hand or the hand strikes the ball. If the ball strikes the hand, even if it lands in front of the player's feet, no penalty should be called. Should this happen right in front of the goal, however, be very sure and perhaps take into account whether it happens to an offensive or a defensive player. When the hand strikes the ball, even if it is a reflex action and therefore an "unintentional" act as far as the player's state of mind is concerned, it should be called. Again, the referee is not a mind reader.

Obviously, the level of play must have some effect on your judgment. Skilled players rarely commit hands unintentionally. On the other

UNINTENTIONAL HANDLING

hand, even young and inexperienced players should learn when the hand's contact with the ball is penalized. The young player may turn away from a hard shot, and is not to be penalized when the ball strikes him on the elbow. In some competitions, young women are allowed to protect their chests, but they should at least have their hands immobile on the chest, palms inward. Just be consistent in your judgment so players can learn from it.

TAKING FREE KICKS

Most free kicks, once awarded, are routine. The kicking team must not get an advantage from incorrectly placing the ball, and the ball should not be moving, but we should not be nitpicking. If a player bends down to stop the ball with his hand and almost simultaneously plays it to a teammate, there's nothing wrong with that. In that situation, the opposing players are usually not ten yards from the ball, but that's the kicker's choice. If he wants ten yards, he has to tell you. That means two things, The player is asking you to hold up play, and often the opponents will set a wall as you motion them back. The closer we are to the penalty area, the greater the tendency of players to seek an advantage to which they are not entitled. It's only your know-how and your firmness that will make sure that the procedure is orderly and fair.

Setting the Wall

First of all, be sure to let the players know that to resume play they must wait for another signal. No one should be allowed to touch the ball in the interim. Move players back by voice and hand signals while stepping off ten yards. If you do that, turn your body in such a way as to keep your eye on the ball and the players at the same time. Especially do not allow the offending team to be provocative by picking up the ball and holding it. If any player is deliberately delaying, caution that player if necessary to let everyone know that your patience is not unlimited. If players on the kicking team try to muscle into the wall, don't allow it. They, of course, don't have to be ten yards from the ball so there should be plenty of room for them. Always remember that it was the other team that created the situation in the first place, however, so don't let them have any advantage. For example, your restart whistle is not a signal for them to come storming forward to block the kick. Only the kick itself can restart play. If the kick is taken prematurely, on the other hand, order a re-kick, regardless of whether the kick scored or not. The ball was dead. The way you deal with these situations will go far toward establishing yourself. Again, it's not a matter of preserving your ego but of being just and fair to both sides and retaining control.

THE PENALTY KICK

A penalty kick (Law XIV) is awarded for any of the ten direct free-kick offenses *committed by the defense inside the penalty box.* In practice, of course, it isn't quite that simple. We are sometimes told that "a foul is a foul" anywhere on the field, but no serious referee can buy that oversimplification and survive. In some 70 to 80 percent of cases, the penalty kick results in a goal, so the foul has to be one that is likely to directly influence the outcome of the game. My own rule of thumb is to award penalty kicks only for fouls that ruin a very good scoring opportunity or are flagrant enough to warrant a caution or ejection. If the attacker has already passed or shot the ball and then is tripped or shoved, let play go on. We must remember that in the penalty box more players are competing for the ball on fewer square yards. Attackers will use all of their skills and tricks to score, while defenders will literally defend their turf with all their might. It doesn't have to become mayhem, but it comes down to this: the attacker in the box must expect to be seriously challenged for the ball. Once, when a center forward complained to me about being muscled a bit (he said "pushed" of course), I said to him: "A player as good as you has to expect to get a lot of attention from his opponents!" That flattered him, and he did not complain again.

It should go without saying that a penalty kick is basically the referee's call. In most cases, the referee will be in a good position to call the play. Linesmen should signal a foul in the penalty box only when the referee is screened from the play and the linesman himself sees the foul clearly as being intentional and having thwarted a good scoring chance. His signal should be simple and unostentatious: a quick wave with the flag and pointing it to the ground before him while moving toward the goal line. Avoid flamboyant waving of the flag while jumping up and down. Assist the referee. Don't force him into a call he does not want to make.

Taking Penalty Kicks

After you have blown the whistle while pointing to the penalty spot, be very deliberate and act as if this was an obvious call. Try to calm down protests without seeming to be defensive. Don't be too quick to caution or eject a player for dissent or vigorously protesting your call, unless he questions your integrity or insults your mother. Remember, the game may be on the line. Place the ball on the spot and tell the player who takes the kick to wait for a signal. See to it that the other players are outside the box and the ten-yard arc, and *behind the ball* (this is a recent addition). The goalkeeper should have both feet on the goal line. Your leading linesman will be on the goal line near the goalkeeper's box, and your best position as referee is about ten yards from the goal line on the opposite side — from there you can see the kick being taken and also watch for possible encroachment. Now give the signal and let justice be done — it often feels like an execution. Although it is not specified in Law XIV, the kick should be taken in a continuous motion. In other words, no elaborate fake or stutter step to throw off the goalkeeper may be used. This unwritten rule is still violated sometimes, even in international play. If a goal is scored in this manner, the referee should order a retake.

Be ready for a parried ball by the goalkeeper or a ball bouncing into the field off the post or the crossbar as players from both teams charge into the box the moment the ball has been played. Be sure it isn't the kicker himself who plays the ball a second time, unless it has first been touched by another player.

The Shoot-out

In a "shoot-out" with penalty kicks taken from the mark, the organization is slightly different. The referee decides which of the goals will be used. A coin toss decides which team will kick first. Players eligible to participate are gathered at midfield with no fixed order required, and the trailing linesman usually has the task of managing the proper alternating of kicks and backing up the referee in keeping score.

In the previous section we discussed the intricacies of encroachment or other forms of interference by either team as the penalty kick is taken. It amounts to this: Do not penalize slight encroachment with re-takes, unless that encroachment has led to an unfair advantage for one team by either scoring a goal or preventing one.

One sometimes controversial feature that remains is illegal movement by the goalkeeper. According to Law XIV, he must stand "without moving his feet" on the goal line until the ball is kicked forward. There is no rule in soccer that is violated more often without being penalized, except the four-step rule. Only if the goalkeeper's motion was flagrant and he made the save should the referee order a retake. During World Cup 1994 I saw few penalty kicks taken, including those that decided three games by shoot-outs, at which the goalkeeper did not move early to dive toward a corner. No one complained. Apparently the international soccer community has silently agreed not to enforce the rule too strictly. Is this an instance of the Spirit of the Law overriding the letter?

I don't know, and no official instructor can publicly state anything but what the law says. The fact is, however, that, in the way soccer has been played all over the world for many decades, the goalkeeper is given some leeway. He gets his chance. Granted it is a bit untidy, but since I have stressed the need for universal consistency in applying the laws, I tend to follow the common practice.

Even when not in Rome, do as the Romans do!

6

Troubleshooting

A SUCCESSFUL REFEREE HAS ALL THE QUALITIES WE have talked about thus far: a love of the game, a good disposition, respect for players, knowledge of the letter and the spirit of the *Laws of the Game*, and experience in applying them. However, success is not only a matter of knowing and doing the right things. It is just as much a matter of avoiding trouble.

Not all trouble is avoidable, of course. If two teams come at each other with drawn swords, so to speak, playing a grudge match and going at it hard and nasty, there isn't much you can do except mete out discipline from the start. Call it close, try to cajole — "Hey, guys, we all have to go to work tomorrow"— and hope that they will settle down. If coaches and captains cooperate, you may be able to complete the game without serious fights or injuries. In a highly competitive game on the college or adult level, you have little choice of staying with the game to the bitter end, unless the game gets out of hand completely. In lower level games you may choose to terminate the game a bit sooner because neither the game nor the participants are well served by allowing a chaotic game to be completed at all costs. Your decision will send a message, especially to young players. You will of course send a complete report to the league or state association. The rest of the day you will fret and wonder if this situation might have been avoided if you had done things differently. We have all had such games, followed by an evening of self-examination and perhaps troubled sleep.

Try to be objective. Don't assume that you did something wrong. Don't assume that you did everything right, either. That's where some guidelines about avoiding trouble may be useful.

Always Be Close to the Play

Use your *experience* and your *condition* to be close enough to sell your call. A call made from thirty yards away is difficult to sell. Your credibility with players rests to a large extent on your being right there. Some referees seem to be in good condition, but they don't use it. It isn't always laziness or carelessness. More often, in my experience, we are so concentrated on what's going on that we are just watching and forget to run at the same time. But the play is moving and so must you. Positioning is half the game.

Presence lends conviction! I have found that to be especially important for linesmen. If you are exactly on line with the last defender, your offside call will usually go unchallenged. But if you are only three yards off, your credibility suffers, and properly so because you are not at a ninety degree angle to the play. The same thing holds true for calls on the goal line: goal kick, corner, or play on? Often you can't make that call properly unless you have followed the play all the way down the line. The very next moment you may have to sprint back again to stay up with the defense when they move out fast. That's when your condition is tested!

Show a Sense of Proportion

Don't be too finicky about the little stuff, such as whether the ball is exactly in position for a free kick or whether it touches the line; whether a player's shirt has come out of his shorts (unless it's the latest fad); incidental contact between two players skirmishing for the ball; or enforcing the four-step rule for the goalkeeper too strictly. Those things irritate players unnecessarily and they will begin to wonder how well you know the inside game. That causes trouble.

Deal Promptly with Bad Sportsmanship

There are a lot of irritating things players will do to provoke their opponents:

◆   Talking trash and taunting opposing players;

◆   Acting as if it's their kick or throw-in, walking away with the ball for ten yards and then sort of throwing it back or just dropping it when you warn with the whistle;

◆   Playing the ball after the whistle;

◆   Trying to distract opponents by making noises behind their backs;

◆   Using delaying tactics such as pretending not to hear the whistle;

◆   Questioning your call or non-call by appealing dramatically to heaven, even if they say nothing.

You can let a little of that sort of thing pass, but not all the time and not by the same players. Warn them, and if it doesn't work, card them. Such discipline will get you respect from the other players as long as you don't sound vindictive. Don't threaten, "If you do that again, I'm going to card you." For one thing, you leave yourself without an option that way. For another, some players will just test you, and that will make things worse.

Anticipate Problems

When you are driving to a game involving a team with whom you have had a problem in the past, prepare yourself mentally. Ask yourself if you handled the situation as well as possible last time. Did you keep your cool? Use the right language? Get the cooperation you needed from a captain or other players? Build a new scenario for yourself to handle any recurrence. Get rid of grudges. This is a new game!

If the problem was with a coach, be sure to greet him or her pleasantly, without a word about past problems. The coach may already have done what you did: reconsider the situation. When you check in players and come to a problem player, give no hint that you remember him. The first time he commits a foul, handle it like any other infraction. If he challenges you verbally, say something like, "Hey, that was last time. Let's not get into that again." It may defuse the situation. After that, don't hesitate to show him a card, if that's the only language he understands. Meanwhile, be sure that nothing between you and that player or coach affects the way you call the game or deal with other players. They know what's going on and they will respect you. Ask a captain to help you keep this player in line, or when you pass by the bench, say to the coach, "I think number 16 needs to sit down for a while." A good coach will then substitute for that player. These are things that have worked for me in the past. You may find your own solutions, but you have to sit down with yourself and think about such situations in advance.

Taking Time Out?

You may sometimes wish that you could take a moment to talk to the players. Such stoppages are not generally part of the game, however. Yet the one time I did just that, it was very successful. In a high school play-off game with too much fouling and bad sportsmanship, and after several yellow and red cards, I called time, gathered the captains and coaches as well as my linesmen at midfield, and said, "Gentlemen, I need your help. If things go on the way they are, I'm afraid we'll have serious injuries, so I'm considering terminating the game. Please take two minutes to talk to your players and ask them to play soccer." That turned the game around completely. Both teams concentrated on the game and scored several good goals. The coaches thanked me for saving the game and their players' health. It might never work again, so I won't advocate it as a general strategy. Certainly it has no place in adult competition. Still, on rare occasions it might be used as a next-to-last resort. The last resort is, of course, terminating the game.

The Right Touch with Players

During the game, only team captains should be allowed to address the referee — and only the referee, not the linesmen. The referee communicates primarily with his whistle and with an occasional direction or warning: Play the ball! Ten yards, please! Wait for the whistle! Take it easy! There can be more or less of this, depending on the game, but be careful. If you talk too much, you are giving the players implicit permission to talk to you and to comment on your calls or complain. If a team captain asks you what you called, simply tell him but don't explain or argue.

Now let us qualify this warning and caution you against appearing haughty and unapproachable. A little remark in a moment of relaxation during a dead-ball situation will let players know that you are human. There is room for laughter, and it's OK to show admiration for a great play, as long as you do it both ways. At the toss, show players that you are looking forward to a good game and that you expect them to have fun too. Don't preach to them about special things you will be watching for, or threaten them with what you will do if. . . . Ask the captains not to approach you while the ball is in play. Request their support in keeping the game moving smoothly, and thank them after the game when they thank you. Remember, you are not natural adversaries. It's their game, and you are there simply to help them have a fair game.

Dissent from the Sidelines

Some trouble can start on the sideline, coming from players on the bench, the coach, or from spectators. Coaches, especially in school and youth soccer, have a demanding and often thankless job. They deserve our respect and cooperation at all levels of the sport. Remember that they are under pressure too. Nonetheless, during the game their role must remain limited. The *Laws of the Game* did not even mention coaches until 1994, when a clause was inserted to allow coaches to give their players directions from the coaching area as long as it is not loud or abusive or otherwise interferes with the game. We should remember that soccer is different from such traditional American sports as baseball, basketball, and football. In those sports, a coach can always catch a referee's ear and express his displeasure. We have all witnessed the distasteful scene of a baseball manager and an umpire hotly arguing a routine call chest to chest, with the spittle flying, before the coach turns away or is ejected from the game. In baseball that's part of the game. Not in soccer! Referees should not allow coaches to shout at them or to run up and down the sideline  ranting and raving, even if it is aimed at their own players. Players don't like it either because it distracts them from the game. Soccer coaches who go berserk should be asked to take a seat a hundred yards away, and the incident should be part of the referee's game report.

Dealing with Spectators

You may have noticed: all spectators are referees, except that you have a whistle and they don't . . . . Spectators can see from sixty yards away the unintentional hands you did not call, and they can judge whether the ball was completely over the goal line or not. If a game is played in a stadium, you have no choice but to ignore the screaming of fans, nasty as they may be. They have paid for their tickets and the right to abuse referees, something these decent citizens would never do in any other setting. Close your ears if you can and don't encourage them by reacting in any visible way. Rabid fans thrive on that.

If the game is being played in a public park or on school grounds, the situation may be more stressful. When parents and other spectators on the sideline use profanity or make threats, you must ask the coach to help you maintain order and common courtesy. The coach by now should be as annoyed as you are. If this doesn't work, tell the coach calmly that his side has two minutes to comply or you will terminate the game. Don't get into a shouting match. One of your linesmen should be close enough to witness the scene. If you have to terminate the game, leave together with your linesmen. Ask them to write their own separate game reports with as much specific information as possible. Don't say anything about forfeits — that's the league's or school authorities' business.

Can We Change?

Unfortunately, we seem to encounter these scenarios often in youth games, which make up some 80 percent of all soccer games. Ironically, that is precisely where we hope that participation in a team sport will teach young people responsibility and good sportsmanship. One problem is that soccer is still a relative newcomer here. Many parents and some coaches have no background in the game and do not know the rules very well. Here, as elsewhere in life, ignorance breeds contempt: the less people know, the more they feel at liberty to express their opinion. Referees have a role to play in saving our sport from such excesses both by their actions and their poise. But schools and clubs could also do a lot to improve the situation. They could organize open meetings at which experienced referees are invited to explain the finer points of the rules and of soccer customs. A coach could invite a referee to come to a team practice before the season and talk about things such as offside, dangerous play, and obstruction. Most of us believe that what young people learn in competitive sports is important for how they will live their lives. We also know that they will take their cues from adults.

I once commended a college hockey coach for always being a model of self-control during games, and he said, "If I complain about the refereeing, I will only hurt the team. My players will also begin to complain instead of concentrating on the game, and the refs certainly won't give us a break, so it's simply common sense." I know that this coach is not just calculating the cost and benefits of good behavior, however. He is a gentleman and his teams are winners. They have been league champions for three years in a row.

Stuff happens, but most of it is created by people.

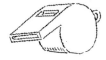

Halftime

My long-time colleague Dick Burns in Colorado Springs showed the yellow card to a player. The fellow took it from his hand and said, "Thank you, sir." Dick reached into his breastpocket again, pulled out the red and said, "You're welcome, but I've got this one too!"

Another colleague, John White, after being told to "Call it both ways, ref!" shook his head and said, "I can't. I have only one whistle."

Heard somewhere about Paul Avis, referee instructor from Toronto: "All a referee needs to know is when to blow the whistle and how to restart play. It's as simple as that."

If you make a mistake, one team will hate you. If you try to make up for it, both teams will.

Referees can afford to close their ears but not their eyes.

Don't break up a fight. Just keep good score.

Let's remember the famous baseball umpire's reply to a batter
who said, "That's a ball":
"Son, it ain't nothin' till I say it is."

A high school player shouts: "Come on, ref, give us a break!" The
referee pulls out the yellow card and points to the bench, saying:
"Sure, go sit down for a while."

A well-known but aging referee to his linesmen before the game:
"Anything in the circle is mine, the rest is yours."

An ancient proverb that may apply to referees and linesmen: "One fool
can cause more trouble than a dozen wise men can fix."

Player: "Ref, you must be blind!"
Ref (pulling the yellow): "You're right, but my hearing is pretty good!"

"It has always been my policy not to comment on referees and I'm
certainly not going to make an exception for this idiot." British
manager quoted in *Football Is Still a Funny Game*

7

The Team: Referees and Linespersons

FIFA HAS RECENTLY DECIDED TO REFER HENCEFORTH in all its publications to linesmen as assistant referees. The change was made, it is said, to achieve gender-neutral language and to add to the stature of the linespersons. To our ears it sounds nonetheless awkward because it seems to assign ranks to referees, when the reality is that all of us are certified referees who work the middle in some games and assist the referee as linesmen or lineswomen in others. We should not be surprised, therefore, if the linesman/lineswoman designation is retained in ordinary usage for some time. Regardless of rank or gender, whether in any given game we are in the middle or on the line, we must recognize our different functions to be important and work together as equals and as a team. We cannot serve the game well without making that commitment.

Pre-game Instructions

We may come to a game directly from our jobs or homes at different places and we do not always know who our colleagues will be. Sometimes we have to hurry from other fields and previous games at different times. Only rarely do we enjoy the privilege of meeting at our leisure in a dressing room with time to discuss our assignments. Thus our teamwork cannot begin until we meet on the field, but that should be all the more reason to take our pre-game arrangements seriously. I remember a number of situations in which referees were careless in checking signals because they knew each other and overlooked some details that came to plague them during the game. We must be professionals who do the job right even if it is a game for boys or girls under age twelve.

Whenever possible, referee and linespersons should go over the instructions and signals at some distance from the field. If you are the referee, you should have a pre-game checklist at least in your head. You should be selective in using the items on your list according to the experience of your linesmen. You don't want to appear condescending. Then enter the field together and go about your business. First impressions count. The referee has assigned different tasks to the linesmen such as helping with checking in players, or checking the balls, the nets, and the condition of the field. In the majority of games that most of us work, there is no time for the referee to do all these things himself. Conditions are seldom perfect, but that is not an excuse for being careless.

You are a team. That applies equally when you work as a referee with club linesmen who don't know your routines. Whoever the lines-

THE REF TEAM

men are, once you are agreed on clear signals, there should rarely be a need for sideline conferences. Such interruptions only tend to signal to players and spectators that you are disagreeing about a call, which takes away from your authority. Linesmen, in turn, should be reluctant to call the referee over, unless it is for something he could not see, such as a serious foul behind his back. If possible, they should wait for a natural stoppage of play.

On the Line

Linespersons should have a clear understanding that the referee should always have the first crack at calling an infraction and that he should not be interfered with if he has a clear view of the play. A linesman is there solely to support the referee, not to correct him. If the referee looks to him, the linesman can give an unobtrusive signal with his free hand to indicate, say, the direction of the free kick, upfield or downfield. He should avoid ostentatiously flapping the flag for a goal kick or corner kick from the far side of the field, when often the referee is in a better position to see who last touched the ball. Have you ever noticed how restrained the linesmen are in professional games? The same thing goes for a close play at the goalmouth: did the ball go in or not? If it didn't, the linesman should do nothing. If in his opinion a goal has been scored, he should quickly turn, perhaps give an unobtrusive agreed-upon signal, and move back up the field as usual. Generally, the initiative for a consultation should come from the referee.

If the linesman disagrees with the referee's call or non-call, he should certainly refrain from shaking his head or responding to a player's inquiry. Once the referee has made a call, he should signal with his flag only if he detected, say, a prior offside and it's important. Not even that, of course, if the referee awarded a free kick to the defense anyway. An overzealous linesperson can make things very difficult for the referee. Not so long ago, a linesman called me over after a ball passed the goal line and said, "I just thought I ought to tell you that number 8 was offside." I asked him why he had not raised the flag if it was important. "Well, I thought I'd leave it to you," he said. "So why didn't you?" I replied with some exasperation and restarted the game with my original call while trying to ignore the questioning looks of players. If there had been no call in the first place, the situation would have been even more embarrassing, and I would have had to restart with a drop ball. On another occasion, in a tense playoff game requiring my full concentration, the linesman raised the flag just as the goalkeeper punted the ball upfield. Wondering what he might have seen, I stopped play and walked over, only to have him tell me that the keeper had taken five steps with the ball. I was tempted to dismiss him right then and there. The moral of these stories is: Let the referee call his own game! In fact, I generally end my instructions to linesmen before important games by saying, "Just be the kind of linesman for me that you would like to have if you were the referee." That says it all.

In return, as a referee you should respect your linesmen. If you know

them well, there should be no need to work through a list of twelve checkpoints every time you work together. If you must overrule a linesman, do it quickly and decisively, and perhaps reward him with an A-OK gesture. You will reap the benefits the next time. Remember that the linesman is a referee in his own right, or he would not be there.

If you are a veteran referee running a line for a less experienced colleague, be especially careful not to undermine his authority with frequent flags or gestures of disapproval. It's his game even if he messes up. The "do unto others" principle applies here also, difficult as it may be.

Linesmen should not take charge of pre-game arrangements unless the referee is very late. When I have been assigned to referee a game, I like to have a chance to check in the teams together with the linesmen. In that way I am establishing first contact with the players: they can size me up, and I get a sense of their mood and attitudes that may help me in the game. If the game is important to them, it should also be important to me, regardless of their age, sex, or level of play. The style and tone of my pre-game routine assures them of that.

Substitute Linesmen

You have a different problem when it's game time and you are short one linesman. Under USSF rules you are obliged to appoint a club linesman. Ask each coach if there is a certified referee among the spectators on his side. If not, find another volunteer who is recommended and seems knowledgeable and assign him limited duties that may or may not include calling offsides. By all means be tolerant and courteous toward that person and include his or her name and service in your game report. Again, under USSF rules you are not allowed to referee the game on the dual control system with the one qualified linesman serving as a referee. If one of the teams should protest the game, both you and the linesman would be in trouble. You also run the risk of being held liable in court should there be a serious injury in that game. In all procedural matters, follow the rules.

This particular rule does not apply to high school games. In fact, the opposite principle applies: no unauthorized person is allowed to serve in an official capacity, but the dual system is allowed. Thus your certified linesman may become the second referee. If you are the only registered high school referee, the best you can do is to ask the coaches to raise a hand when the ball goes out of bounds and hustle up and down the field by yourself. Usually it works out quite well, though I always ask captains not to play the offside trap. A team can live but also die by it.

The Dual System

Worldwide, the diagonal system of control has long been the standard. When I began refereeing, the two-man system was used widely in high schools and colleges, partly because of a dearth of referees but in many cases also because it was preferred by American educators. Two whistles, it was thought, do more good than one for proper game control. Some referees who grew up with that system still prefer it. It is more prestigious and more fun to have your own whistle than to be subservient to another referee. How often have we ourselves not been impatient while running the line, wishing that we had a whistle to deal with a situation that escaped the referee? It's only human.

The two-man system sometimes appears simpler. Each referee has his own line and his own territory, and between them they overlook the entire field at times. You do not get caught way behind a fast break after a corner kick, your back is covered, and you can always be in place to make the offside call. If two people learn to work together well, there is no more problem of conflicting signals than one may experience between a referee and his linespersons. When things get difficult for one referee in hard-played games, the two-man system can sometimes help you to lessen the pressure that one referee would experience. Using the dual system, I have often experienced good teamwork with many referees, giving my colleague a split second to make a call when the play is closer to him but not hesitating when a foul needs to be called and my partner is partly screened from the play. Some referees don't like to have another referee "mess up" their game, but I suspect that such people are not very good at working together with linesmen either. They like to be boss.

A good team of referees is not concerned with who's in charge but with the best possible way of conducting a fair game together. The two-man system is not the best way. I would guess that 70 percent of play for the ball takes place in an inside rectangle of 50 x 80 yards on a field that is, say, 75 x 110 yards. That means that in the two-man system neither referee is closer than 20 yards to most of the plays. The principle that *presence lends conviction* cannot operate here. To be sure, most of us who have experience with the dual system have learned to "pinch in" when the ball gets into the penalty area, but that is not enough. You may not see the subtle shirtpull or elbow in midfield from the sideline or hear what players are calling each other. Also, when one referee is more experienced or more dominating than his partner, he will tend to take over the game, and players will begin to appeal to him to make the call that they think his partner should have made. Unfortunately, in many cases that referee will do just that. It's simply not a healthy situation.

The Diagonal System

In the three-person system, a good center referee brings presence and consistency to the game. He never runs a simple diagonal. He is going to be all over the field, wherever his presence is required. He observes the diagonal only to the extent of wanting to be in full view of one of his linesmen at all times. He asks his linesmen to get fully involved in the game because he needs their support. When I have good linesmen, I know I'm going to have a good game. Together we can almost produce a masterpiece! If the linesmen are inexperienced or weak, I know I have to be doubly alert, run more, and I will feel greater pressure to keep things running smoothly. But even then, I prefer the three-man system. I'm sure players and coaches do, too.

Alternate Systems

It has been argued that the field is too big, the modern game too fast, and the players too sophisticated for just one referee to handle. Some students of the game have suggested two referees and two linesmen. In my opinion, that would create a surfeit of judges even at the highest level. This isn't American football, and the linesmen would have practically no other function than flagging out-of-bounds.

The 1996–97 high-school rule book permits the use of the "three-whistle" system of control. That seems to me like overkill. The high school game as such does not require it. It would only produce more tension and controversy.

If the diagonal system places too much of a burden on the center referee, I can think of only one reasonable solution: to give more responsibility to linesmen. They don't need a whistle, but they should be encouraged to signal more often for fouls that occur close to them and that the referee may not be able to see clearly. They have been trained to be referees, so let us build on that. We will have to train referees to have confidence in their linesmen and allow the linesmen to assist the referee more actively than tradition has permitted. The fortunate part of this is that it won't require a change in the rules. The referee will still make the final decision.

As an emeritus referee for the last ten years, I have learned to become more dependent on linesmen, and I am certain that it has helped my game. I have also run more lines than before. I used to think that I could see it all as a referee. Now I know better. What's more important: it has helped the game that the players are having and that belongs to them.

Does all of this need saying? If you are a referee, you have probably shared many of these insights. But I think that all of us referees and linespersons can do with an occasional reminder about the importance of correct game procedures, of knowing ourselves, and of the people skills it takes to work games together smoothly.

A chain is as strong as its weakest link.

Football flourished in Britain throughout the Middle Ages in rural villages as well as among students and other city-dwellers. Often, authorities tried to restrict the game on account of the bloody battles that were fought between towns or neighborhoods. A proclamation by King Edward II in 1314 forbade the game "for as much as there is a great noise in the city caused by hustling over large balls . . . on pain of imprisonment." Further attempts to ban the game were made by Richard II, Henry IV, and Elizabeth I, apparently without success. Their view of football was expressed by pamphleteer Philip Stubbs, who wrote in his *Anatomy of Abuses* in 1583, about players who "dash [the opponent] against the hart with their elbow, butt him under the short ribs with gripped fists and a hundred such murdering devices." Still, there were voices like that of a man named Mulcaster, who praised the benefits of football because it "strengtheneth and brawneth the whole body, and by provoking superfluities downward, it dischargeth the head and upper parties, is good for the bowels, and [drives] downe the stone and gravell from both the bladder and the kidnies." In the long run, the view of football as healthful prevailed.

8

Youth Soccer:
The New Breed

WHAT IS THE SECRET OF SOCCER'S RAPID GROWTH IN
America? Twenty years ago the number of registered youth soccer players in the U.S. was, according to U.S. Youth Soccer Association
(USYSA) figures, 127,000. Ten years later there were 1.2 million, and the
1995 figure was 2.4 million. A Soccer Industry Council report estimates
that 18.2 million people age six and older, of whom 7 million are female
and 11.2 million male, play soccer in the U.S. That staggering figure must
include the many thousands of youths who play in programs organized

by city recreation departments or by the YMCA and other associations such as the American Youth Soccer Organization (AYSO). On city playgrounds these days, on the beach, or in summer camps, we are more likely to see kids kicking a soccer ball around than throwing a baseball. Young children can kick a ball without frustration long before they can throw or catch one. That is at least one answer to our question. The game re-quires little more than a ball, and anyone can play. In fact, a tin can will do. From there, it is only a few steps to goals made of pipes, homemade flags, and colored T-shirts and sneakers. Move a few larger steps beyond that, and we are at the colorful scene of the Pikes Peak Invita-tional Tournament held each June in the

magnificent setting of the U.S. Air Force Academy in Colorado Springs with more than 250 youth teams from all over the United States and Canada playing on twenty-eight fields for five days.

Such a display is a measure of the enthusiasm, dedication, and orga-nizational skills of parents, coaches, club officials, and not least the 170 referees who sacrifice some of their vacation time. It is also a measure of the tremendous expenditures made for travel, housing, meals, and tour-nament fees. For better or worse, in this country, soccer is a middle-class sport, a product of suburbia. While there are no color lines in soccer, the relative lack of social and racial diversity in soccer reflects clearly the existing demographic patterns in regions and neighborhoods. Yet, the basic simplicity of soccer and its relatively low equipment cost should make it accessible to all young people, as it is the world over. It is a goal worth pursuing.

There is reason to believe that soccer will soon match the older popular sports in America such as baseball and basketball. Whether soccer will also gain similar attention from millions of spectators and from the media, and compete with equal success for the sports dollar, remains uncertain. For those of us who measure a sport's success primarily in terms of participation and social values such as promoting health and teaching kids to function in groups and acquire values such as fairness and sportsmanship, however, soccer is already a great success.

Implications for Referees

The dramatic growth of youth soccer certainly affects referees. First of all, we have to recruit large numbers of referees to cover the thousands of youth games played both at the recreational level and in state and regional competitions under the auspices of USYSA and AYSO, as well as in the schools. Fortunately, these programs have been able to draw upon parents as referees. It would be interesting to know how many of the more than 70,000 certified soccer referees in the U.S. became referees because of the involvement of their children. For the same reason, unfortunately, many of them tend to leave the sport as soon as their children finish high school. Yet, with the steadily rising skill level of players, we need to build a much larger reserve of younger referees who choose refereeing as a long-term commitment and who aspire to move up in the ranks of referees through periodic assessments. Older referees should encourage them to make that commitment.

It is also time for us to develop a more conscious philosophy of refereeing youth soccer. Some of our colleagues act as if youth soccer is just like adult refereeing, only easier. In my experience, nothing is farther from the truth. To be sure, adult players tend to be more subtle and calculating in their fouling than youthful players, and their individual duels may be more physical because of their greater size and strength. Experienced players quickly learn what a particular referee is calling and what they can get away with, and they will adjust their play accordingly. In youth soccer the challenges for referees are of a different kind. Although the quality of play has improved tremendously over the last ten years, the younger players differ a lot in terms of their aggressiveness and physical output. They are more easily confused and frustrated by different styles and standards of refereeing. They are more sensitive to being called for fouls when they intended no evil, so they may easily become distraught.

Young players are also very sensitive to the sideline commentary of well-meaning spectators who do not know the game well. Some, especially mothers, are very protective of their offspring and feel that the

referees allow too much physical contact. Fathers, on the other hand, often like to see their children, especially their sons, be aggressive and encourage them to "take out" an opponent. Coaches, too, can become quite vociferous. Young players sometimes stand around and do not react well to sudden shifts in play. Coaches know that in youth play, where ball skills are still limited, many games are won or lost on hustle and intensity, so they try to fire up their young players.

The young often suffer from these pressures and from the constant shouts of "Do this — Don't do that — Oh, not again! — How can you miss that?" We have seen eleven-year-olds crying because their team was one goal behind with fifteen minutes still to play! Referees, therefore, should avoid adding to those pressures. Rather, the younger players are, the more we need to be understanding, explain things, and take off the sharp edges. Even an occasional request to coaches and parents to tone things down is not out of order. Some youth leagues and teams have successfully introduced an agreed-upon "silent quarter," a period during which only words of praise and encouragement are to be heard from the sideline.

Discipline

It is unfortunate that the majority of cases before disciplinary boards such as protested games or misconduct by spectators or coaches come from the youth divisions, and more often from the younger age groups than from the older ones. That should make us wonder about our perspective on sports for youth. Foreign visitors are often astounded at the competitive atmosphere surrounding our youth games and at seeing complete teams of certified referees officiating in games for ten-year-olds and being paid for it. If competent referees can be found to serve the game in this way, it would seem unfair to question their contribution, but it is not improper to emphasize the need for a sense of proportion. Sometimes it seems that the more formal we try to be in our organization of youth games, the more frequent are the complaints and protests. Many referees have the experience that games they have had to referee without linespersons are usually very peaceful, if only because people know that not everything can be perfect. Ironically, it also seems to make it easier for the referee to concentrate on a job that is his, and his alone. Although this cannot possibly apply to premier youth leagues and players from, say, fifteen up, it is good to be reminded that a youth game is not a professional match.

If I have from time to time seemed to portray parents and coaches in a harsh light, that is not my general view. I am as often delighted with their enthusiasm and mature judgment as I have been indignant about their occasional lack of understanding of what we are trying to accomplish. Referees can through their own demeanor demonstrate to them that, particularly in youth soccer, the game belongs to the players.

Today's children are tomorrow's adults.

9

Women:
The Fresh Breeze

ONE OF THE MOST EXCITING ASPECTS OF THE GROWTH of soccer has been women's participation in the game in many parts of the world. The U.S. has played a major role in that development. A 1995 report shows a total of 32 million women players registered in 102 countries, compared with 140 million male players worldwide. The official number for the U.S. alone was six million women players. The first World Championship for women, held in 1961 in China, was won by the United States. The general consensus among analysts called the American women's team a model in style of play and competitiveness for other countries. The second championship, played four years later in Sweden, showed a general improvement in skills and tactics. This time, Norway beat Germany in the finals, and the U.S. team beat China for third place. The strongest areas for women's soccer at present are, as reflected in these results, Europe, the U.S., and Asia. The expected development of women's soccer in South America, Africa, and Australia will undoubtedly add a lot to the luster and quality of future women's world championships.

Just as important as the increase in teams and players is the rising number of women referees and the growing opportunities for them to referee at higher levels. The first woman to officiate at a professional

soccer game was Betty Ellis, who in 1981 served as a lineswoman in a NASL match between the San Jose Earthquakes and the Edmonton Drillers. Real progress at this level came gradually, however. In the 1991 world championship for women, a small number of female referees was used, mostly as lineswomen. In 1994 FIFA's Referees' Committee nominated six female and six male referees, as well as six linespersons of each gender to officiate at the twenty-six games held in Sweden in 1995. The championship final was refereed by a team of women. One member of this select group of female referees was Leann Hepburn, a schoolteacher from Denver. At the 1996 Olympic Games, where women's soccer was introduced for the first time, the original plan was to have only women referee women's games. Unfortunately, that was not done although female referees did participate. Increased opportunities for women to referee in both men's and women's games at high levels should become a priority.

Women have for a long time been active on the international scene in sports such as track and field, swimming, tennis, gymnastics, and skating and skiing. The addition of team sports has been a more recent phenomenon. The 1996 Olympic Games in Atlanta saw women's teams compete in basketball, beach volleyball, field hockey, indoor volleyball, team handball, softball, and soccer. The greatest impetus for women's team sports came in 1972 with the passing by Congress of Title IX, which required equal opportunity in schools and colleges. As a result, the participation of girls as a percentage of all students who played soccer in secondary schools rose from 9.1 percent in 1975–76 to 30 percent in 1985–86 and 42.5 percent in 1995–96. In the past ten years, the number of women's varsity soccer teams at the college level has tripled. While some sports for women still experience discrimination with regard to available funds and facilities in the schools and colleges, one can readily see the continuing adjustments and improvements that are being made. Among male administrators and coaches, earlier resistance and condescending attitudes are gradually giving way to open admiration. It's time!

Anyone who wants to see what this revolution has wrought only needs to visit the soccer fields in public parks and on school grounds on any given day or at summer tournaments. In almost any community, thousands of young women are now playing soccer not only with the energy and enthusiasm typical of today's women, but with great skill. Gone are the days when young women ran and threw "like a girl." Obviously, this development cannot be separated from the general increase in women's participation in other fields of endeavor that used to be virtually closed to them. It would be wrong, however, to see women's sports as a mere by-product of that trend. The reverse is also true: women's participation in new sports is quite naturally also giving them the incentive to enter more vigorously into new careers in business and politics. Sports demand the dedication and discipline of the whole person toward the achievement of a goal, often in cooperation with others, and there can be no better preparation for "real life" than the character training provided by sports. This is especially true of team sports such as soccer, in which team work and leadership qualities are of the essence.

Male soccer referees, in turn, have had to gain new insights and learn new social skills required by women's sports. Their reorientation has not always come easily. Here are some do's and don'ts that all of us should observe:

1. Respect women athletes as you would any male player. That means in the first place: Do not give them special treatment — neither special favors nor special rules. As trained athletes, women expect to compete hard and they don't need our well-meant but somewhat condescending protection from contact. Just because a female player goes down, does not mean that you have to blow the whistle immediately and call in a trainer. Apply the "hands" rule just as you would with male players, although age and experience may be a factor, just as it would with boys. And don't accept dissent or the use of foul language from women either. When you show a female player a yellow card, she knows that you take her seriously!

2. Be careful with your own words and gestures. Playful references to a female athlete's dress, let alone to her physical attributes are no-no's. Don't call them "honey" or "sweetheart," even jocularly. Similarly with women coaches. Be pleasant but at the same time businesslike and objective, even if off the field you may be personal friends or colleagues. They will appreciate it.

3. Observe these same rules in working with female referees. Happily, there are more of them now. Many of them have been players and know their stuff. Male referees should resist the urge to lecture them or assist them in a way that only undermines their authority. Instead, they should support them quietly in front of coaches or spectators who sometimes find it difficult to accept a woman in charge.

4. We must work to recruit more women referees for all levels of soccer. Women are *playing* at higher levels, so we should expect them to also break through the barriers in *refereeing* amateur adult and professional soccer games. It will take a lot of effort. Women should also be welcome in administrative bodies and on committees dealing with discipline or rules revision rather than dress codes. We must include them not in order to be fair or to look progressive, but for what they have to offer. The game of soccer can only benefit from this infusion of new energies and perspectives.

Women can blow their whistles, too!

Soccer
the American Way

I S THERE SUCH A THING AS AN "AMERICAN WAY" IN
soccer? Perhaps. For most of this century American soccer was only a
footnote on the world's sport scene. In its relative isolation it developed
its own forms of organization, and in some instances, such as high school
and college soccer, it even had its own rules. In the last decade, however,
and especially since World Cup 1994, the U.S. has become fully recognized among soccer nations of the world. In that World Cup, our national team played very representative soccer, our fans were an example to

the world of the spirit of international sportsmanship, and our referees served as competently as those from other countries. It may be instructive to talk a little about the way and the directions in which soccer has grown in this country, compared with its history in other countries.

Patterns of Development and Organization

In the nineteenth century, England was the cradle of modern soccer, and its patterns of organization spread quickly to other countries. Although one can point to the existence of competitive sports as early as the Middle Ages, when activities such as horseback riding, shooting, and a form of tennis were among the entertainments of the ruling classes, these were typically individual sports. In England there were some rough team sports in which a ball was hurled or kicked by teams from neighboring villages as early as Shakespeare's time. Even today one can see young men in Northern Holland throwing small stone balls along the narrow cobblestone roads with ditches to either side, to decide whose rock will arrive first at some point miles away. Such sporting events are usually celebrated afterwards in the local pub. From the late nineteenth century on, as soccer became popular with the working populations of large industrial cites in

England and elsewhere, it retained some of that character as a popular entertainment for common folk and as a center for social life. In Europe today, even many of the best-known professional soccer teams are part of large sports clubs with other sports divisions. The famous Spanish club Barcelona had 102,000 dues-paying members in 1996. Most young players start in organized soccer with smaller local clubs at age ten to twelve. When they show special promise, they are invited at an early age to join one of the development teams of the larger first-division clubs. School sports play only a minor role in this picture.

In America, the place of a popular mass sport was occupied by baseball. Baseball was played in organized form as early as 1846 and it went fully professional with the founding of the National League in 1871. Other big time team sports were organized and grew into that same mold, though none ever acquired the status of "the game itself," as a local sports reporter calls baseball. We now have the NFL (football), the NBA (basketball) and the NFL (hockey), all organized as franchised corporations owned by one or more wealthy business executives and played by athletes who are themselves millionaires. In these professional sports, the owners and players are in business, which is not to question their love of the game. Players are tagged at high school age or even earlier as showing professional promise. They are sometimes drafted by professional clubs as soon as they finish high school, to be further developed in minor leagues until they make the big leagues or are "washed out." That is one form of apprenticeship. Increasingly, however, especially in football and basketball, such advanced training is provided by colleges and universities into which players are similarly drafted and where they receive payment in the form of "full ride" academic scholarships. This pattern is now taking hold in American soccer as well. All of us know these patterns of sports organization, and they are outlined here only in order to provide a contrast with the growth of soccer and most other sports in England and on the European continent.

Soccer in America has up to now tended to follow the typical development pattern from youth leagues to high school and college. Since World Cup 1994, with the organization of a three-tier system of professional and semiprofessional competition (MLS, A-League, and USISL), that is beginning to change. The USSF will no longer draw directly upon the reservoir of outstanding college players for its national and Olympic teams, but rather on special development squads of selected players just out of high school who will make up the basis for our own professional leagues. As Paul Gardner, the dean of American soccer writers said recently about this shift, "The vision of a stream of exceptional twenty-two-year-old players issuing forth from the colleges, all suitably well-educated . . . is an attractive one. But it has been obvious for quite a while . . . that this is a pipe dream." It is thought that to compete on an international level, players have to play year-round in top competitions. Not surprisingly, this shift is applauded by the owners and coaches of professional teams and deplored by college coaches and educators.

Continued Development

Meanwhile, regardless of the different objectives that people may pursue, American soccer is prospering at all levels. There is competition for boys and girls at all age levels in numerous clubs as well as in schools from ninth grade on. In most cases, club competition is at least statewide, extending to tournaments all over the nation and even tours abroad. Regional and state associations are well-organized. Our youth coaches and referees are usually paid, and parents are expected not only to pay significant dues, but also to give freely of their time in driving their kids' teams to practices and distant competitions. All of these factors combined allow us to expect the continued rise of American soccer in quality and popularity.

The Role of Social Conditions

Unfortunately, as we mentioned earlier, the financial costs and other burdens placed on parents have caused soccer in America to become primarily a suburban middle-class sport. One does not see many children playing soccer on inner-city streets here the way European and South American children do, learning their ball skills and tactical moves without the benefit of coaches and referees. It seems to make them "savvy" and hungry in a way that most young American players are not. Also, they know their adult soccer heroes from the local club or the national team and try to emulate them the way city kids in Chicago or New York emulate Michael Jordan. Are we missing that important element in our soccer picture?

Street Soccer

Colorado's USYSA soccer magazine *Goal Post Scripts* recently reported on a movement to organize "street soccer" in America. The idea is to let young players play their own game without the aid of coaches to teach them ball skills and basic tactics. That should, we are told, help them to develop better scoring skills and imaginative play with the spontaneity and "savvy" we have mentioned. It seems ironic that we are going to organize "unorganized soccer" for our suburban kids in order to match the sand-lot conditions that have produced so many star players in other countries. Understandably, we are drawn by the exciting play of teams from such countries as Nigeria and Cameroon and remember that most of these players developed their skills while playing barefoot on gravel lots with any kind of ball available. But America is a different country. Can we introduce the street soccer pattern when it is not a natural part of our society? Or is street soccer to become a fifteen-minute segment of every practice session? It might be more effective to halt the unfortunate drift toward organizing competition for ever younger players at age six or seven. We might also encourage informal play during the off-season and indoors without the constant benefit of coaches and referees. The results could be interesting.

In America soccer is just one of many popular team sports. We are used to having young people play various sports in their designated seasons, especially in the schools. Athletes are encouraged to "letter" in more than one sport, and generally they have benefited by it. Often they realize only in their late teens which sport best suits their skills and preferences. Interestingly, however, competitive youth soccer is being made into almost a year-round sport, just as it is in other parts of the world. That process may be accelerated when we begin to draw upon the masses of big-city youth. I would like to see such broadened participation not only for the wider reservoir of talent but also for reasons of cultural and economic diversity.

Size and Strength in Soccer

Still another typically American feature is our emphasis on the size of players in practically all sports. Game programs and preseason reports list

the height and the weight of players. Newspaper reports tell us that this 250-pound tackle can run the 40 yards in 4.6 seconds. That makes him, it is thought, "good material." Soccer programs have taken over this practice, which is not found elsewhere in the world. The most prominent world stars in soccer of the last few decades, such as the Brazilian Pele, Franz Beckenbauer of Germany, Johan Cruyff of the Netherlands, Maradona of Argentina, and Rossi of Italy, were not known for their impressive physical stature. Neither are most of the players on our last World Cup team. Soccer stars are recruited for their quickness and ball skills, as well as a "feel" for the game, rather than for their pure speed or size. They do tend to have exceptional body balance, so they are not easily shouldered off the ball. They jump extremely well for high balls, and their anticipation and timing are exemplary. It has been argued that, given equal skills and athletic talent, the big and fast player is always going to be superior. For soccer the question is not so simple. Is the big and powerful player likely to develop all of the subtler soccer skills we have emphasized, or might great size at times be a handicap? One might ask why all these countries in which soccer has been the most popular and developed sport have never considered size and pure speed to be of prime importance. Rather, since the 1950s, international soccer has shifted to an ever greater emphasis on quickness, superior ball skills, and great mobility. The makeup of our national team shows that our top coaches have recognized this, and the assumption is that the national program will have a trickle-down effect on play at all levels. Mere "athleticism" — a favorite media term — won't do it.

Implications for Referees

The present soccer scene in America and our recent FIFA selections show that we have also begun to favor the quick and mobile referee. I hope that those same referees will begin to put more emphasis on protecting young soccer players from physical intimidation in age groups where their physical development is often quite uneven. Too many players are hit just after they release the ball, and too many goalies go down with a high ball not because there was an intentional foul but simply because of heavy incidental contact. Some players are injured by an opponent's 20-foot sliding tackle. Too many "shoulder tackles" are actually hip charges or forms of holding.

Naturally, the level of competition and the age of the players make a difference. At the top level, play can be very physical, but players know what they are doing, and the so-called "professional foul" can be properly penalized by an experienced referee who knows where to draw the line. At lower levels, both in amateur adult and youth soccer, there is still a tendency to play the body and to use one's size and strength in ways that are detrimental to the game. In some youth tournaments involving foreign teams, our guests have remarked on our physical style of play. American players and coaches at the same time are apt to note the more subtle fouls by foreign players such as shirt-pulling, a subtle tap on the ankle, and "accidental" elbows and the like, which are also physical, but appear to be less violent. These infractions are now also on the increase in American soccer, and referees should look out for them. What we said about creating a level playing field must work both ways, and no particular style of play should enjoy an unfair advantage. As players become more sophisticated, not to say devious, referees will have to sharpen their skills as well.

The race is not always to the swift,
nor the battle to the strong.

Football became respectable in England in the 1800's when it was adopted by the famous "public schools" such as Rugby, Eton, and Harrow for its important role in promoting the *mens sana in corpora sano,* i.e. the ideal of a sound mind in a healthy body. Generation after generation of political and military leaders who built the British Empire were educated in these schools in which physical strength and courage were prized as much as intellectual achievements. Such discipline demanded of course that team sports were governed by set rules. The attempts at achieving uniformity led to sharp disagreements between "carriers" and "dribblers." The former insisted that football should allow the ball to be played with the hands and the feet and also permit tackling and "hacking." The "dribblers" advocated a cleaner game in which the ball could be stopped with the hands but played forward only with one's feet, and in which rough tackling was prohibited. A meeting called in Cambridge in 1863 to settle these disputes led instead to a clear separation between "rugby football" and "association football," with the latter becoming popularly known as soccer.

11

The Politics of Refereeing

IN SELECTING THE U.S. TO HOST WORLD CUP 1994, FIFA gave recognition to soccer's arrival as a major sport in this country. It was also a reward for the work of thousands of people at all levels of our sport who made it all possible, including referees. Yet, despite the efforts of the USSF in offering clinics and setting standards for certification and assessment, the number of competent referees to carry the burden of rapid growth remains too small. The total number of certified referees in the U.S. does look impressive: In 1995 there were some 68,000 of us. If we break that figure down into the various grades of certification, however, the problem immediately becomes clear.

> FIFA referees and assistant referees 19
> National referees .... ca. 100
> State referees .... ca. 2,300
> R1 and R2 referees .... over 65,000

The total figure at the end of 1996 was 84,000. A diagram would show a spindly pyramid: very wide at the bottom and extremely thin toward the top. The number of national referees needed for the new professional leagues and national amateur cup games is far below our needs. Likewise, the number of state referees, many of whom cover higher level amateur league games as well as thousands of college games each week in the fall season, is especially small. But even our largest group of R1 and R2 referees is inadequate if we consider the need. Taking the state of Colorado as an example, there are more than 55,000 registered youth players, which amounts to perhaps 3,000 youth teams that compete at least once a week during the fall and spring seasons, in addition to the frequent summer tournaments. Colorado has some 2,200 certified referees ranging from age thirteen to age seventy. Clearly, that number is inadequate to cover all scheduled games properly. In addition, the USSF reports an annual attrition of more than 25 percent, which means there is a high number of inexperienced referees each year to replenish the ranks.

Many referees work three or more youth games on Saturdays, a couple of adult games on Sundays, and several high school or college games during the week. These iron men and women earn our respect, but healthy as it may be for them, it cannot be healthy for the game. One cannot properly concentrate on that many games in a day or a weekend. It is difficult to shift in short order from one set of rules to another and from refereeing a boys' high school game to a men's amateur game, with

a girls' under-twelve game in between. Assigners in a given region are hard-pressed to provide referees for hundreds of games during the weekend, so we cannot blame them for using any referee they can find to work more games than perhaps they ought to. This situation is not the best for the development of new referees. They can become stuck at the lower levels of competition and sometimes feel little incentive to become upgraded to higher levels because they can find more than enough work to keep busy without being formally assessed.

The picture is not altogether gloomy, of course. When on any given Saturday I walk through a complex of a dozen soccer fields with the colorful spectacle of hundreds of young people from ages eight to eighteen enthusiastically chasing the ball, many of them skilled and well coached, I am excited about the future of soccer in America. Naturally, I also watch the referees. The majority of them are either under twenty or over forty, it seems. Where are the potential recruits from the group between twenty and forty whom we need for further development? Many of them are in college or they have just started a career and a family that demand all their time. They may still be playing soccer themselves and that's all they can do.

Potential referees of the young adult generation are not fond of taking orders and they don't like to give them either, especially not to their peers. They wouldn't mind becoming involved, but they also want to be free to go mountain-biking if

the spirit so moves them on a beautiful Sunday morning. Many of them are simply reluctant to become referees because they have seen and heard the abuse that referees must tolerate, particularly in youth soccer, which would be their starting level. Are there things we can do to make refereeing soccer more attractive to that group?

Let's look for possible answers. First, soccer is still not as established in the minds of the public and of athletic directors as many other sports are. Nor does soccer command the respect — and therefore the money — that football or basketball do. This affects both the organization of competition and the atmosphere at soccer games. Referee assigners complain that, while school football schedules are set a year or more in advance, they often have to wait until mid-August before soccer schedules are complete and they can assign referees. Frequent schedule changes — often made for flimsy reasons — force assigners into last-minute scrambling to cover games. At almost all levels, the scheduling of games and the assigning of referees is not as well administered as it is in the more traditional sports. This ought to change, and I think that referee organizations as well as State Soccer Associations and State High School Athletics Boards should use their influence to bring improvement. At the same time, soccer referees and linesmen themselves can do a lot for the image of soccer and its standing by being dependable and by looking and acting the part of professionals. If being a soccer referee earns respect as well as pocket money, it will look more attractive to potential recruits.

Prospects for Improvement

Despite these problems, there are some positive signs. The percentage of state and national referees is gradually rising, and more advanced clinics are being offered. The USSF and state associations also give coaches a chance to upgrade themselves through courses and clinics. Many parents are learning the finer points of the game, too. The hundreds of summer youth tournaments all over the country contribute to a certain standardization of coaching and refereeing. Many youth teams travel and gather a lot of soccer experience even abroad. That is something one wishes referees would have a chance to do also. Soccer is part of a world culture, and all of us ought to have that experience.

Climbing the Ladder

Once you have become a referee, you will want to be the best you can be. You will soon want to move beyond youth and high school refereeing to refereeing adult games in your state and region, and possibly beyond. How far can you go? That is partly a matter of your availability and partly a matter of personal ambition.

In any organized group of people there is the question of who has the most power or influence and how they get it. Fortunately, having authority is not what refereeing is about. Out on the field you may wield

a whistle, but you are not on a power trip. We talked about that in Chapter 1. Then what about the situation off the field? Who gets the good assignments? Some referees think that getting a playoff game or a championship match is "all politics." In some sense that may be true, but it largely depends on *how* you move up, whether it is by merit or by playing politics.

Getting a promotion in your workplace or a seat on the school board involves a bit of subjectivity and word of mouth. Usually it is the outcome of a lot of peoples' observations. In soccer also, the plum assignments generally go to people who have been around the game a long time and have earned the respect of their peers and of players and administrators. The administrators themselves usually get where they are be-cause they are thought to be competent and fair. If you tell me that it's not that way in your own association, I can only suggest that you become active in it. The best thing you can do, however, is to work hard at being the best you can be on the field, and to be a good colleague off it. "Cream will rise to the top," grandmother used to say, and to want to be the best is not an ignoble ambition. In fact, for the further development of soccer we *must* train referees for the highest levels. Coaches and administrators of Major League Soccer argue that even our more experienced referees spend too many years in youth soccer and in high school and college competition to have a feel for the very different challenges and require-ments of professional soccer. And where there are new challenges, there are also rich opportunities.

So How Do You Get There?

We started out by discussing the main qualities of a good referee. We stressed such things as appearance, attitude, and bearing, in addition to knowing the game. It takes all these things to become a National or a FIFA referee. Few of us can have it all, however. I know a very good referee who is well-known, respected, and liked, but you probably won't ever see him in top games because somehow he does not look the part. The Lord did not bless him with a great physique. He is built a little tubby with short legs, and he is balding on top. But he has good eyesight, a great sense of humor, and some cunning as well as good judgment. He does not toot his own horn very much, but he blows a darn good whistle. Coaches and players know that he will give them a good game, and lines-man like to work for him. He has given more to the game than most of us. He has an act on the field that most of us could not imitate or sell, but it works for him! And that is what we should all do: find out what our strengths and weaknesses are and build our own style on that. That will take us a long way.

Besides being a referee, there are many other ways to serve the game and to be recognized: as a referee assigner, an instructor or assessor, as a State Referee Administrator, a newsletter editor, or in some other official capacity. If you have the time and the appetite for it, they will find you.

Twelve Steps

Having said all that, if you love the game and have a healthy amount of energy and ambition, you might go far as a referee. How should you go about it? Here are some of the steps I recommend:

1. Get to know the game by playing it at the highest level you are capable of. There is no substitute for having played the game and having earned some battle scars. You can't really learn soccer well in an armchair or from the stands.

2. Attend your first USSF referee clinic at an early age, even during your playing days. It will help your own game, too. Start doing some reffing in lower youth games. Don't wait for an assigner to call you. Call him yourself. Run some lines at a little higher level and get a feel for what it takes.

3. Watch the best referees and try to get to work with them. Learn from them without copying them. Discuss particular situations that came up.

4. From your first game on, concentrate on the game and forget about coaches and fans. Try to disregard your own emotions too, the flutters in your belly and the indignation when players test you. They will! Act as if your call is the most obvious in the world and don't argue about it. You can think about your mistakes when you get home.

5. Be available as often as you can and do not think you are too good for a lower assignment. The more games you work, the more you will learn.

Some of those lower games may teach you the most. Assigners favor referees who are available to work any games, regardless of the level. And don't think too much about what it pays. Sure, the money comes in handy, but if that is what you do it for, I doubt that you are going to be a successful referee.

6. Always treat your fellow referees with respect, and don't do or say anything that will interfere with their game control or getting the respect of coaches, players, and fans. The golden rule certainly applies here: Do unto others . . . !

7. Read the rule books. Then read them again. And again. You should also be familiar with the USSF's *Referee Administrative Handbook*. Keep a list of the main differences between soccer at different levels in schools, colleges, and amateur leagues. Consult the *Handbook* while you get ready for a game to remind yourself of the substitution rule in this league; of a new procedure for cautions (temporary send-off?); of overtime arrangements (this is post-season, so there may be special rules) and penalty kicks (who is eligible to participate in the shoot-out?); and timing (how long are the halves for this league?). We all make errors of judgment, but you should never get caught in a technical error. Any referee worth his salt has the laws at his fingertips. If you run into special situations, call the rules interpreter when you get home.

8. Go to as many advanced clinics as you can. Take all the tests and find out what your errors were, not just whether you passed.

9. Take the annual condition tests of your association. Stay in shape between seasons and do lots of interval running as well as aerobics to stay loose. Stretch before games — too few of us do, and we pay for it. Fitness is not a matter of how far you **can** run but of how much you **do** run

when it counts. One more little thing: Before you enter the field, screw your head on right.

10. Don't stay local. Go out of town or out of state to referee tournaments, and ask for league assignments out of town so others will get to know you. That's politics, of course, but you also learn how they referee elsewhere, and that is valuable for when you move up and travel around the globe! And look the part when you are a visitor somewhere. Polish your armor. Shine those shoes. Get that haircut. Throw away that faded shirt and buy socks long enough to reach your knees. And after the game, keep your nose clean and stay sober.

11. Keep a record of all your games, not just for renewing your annual license but because you will want to be assessed for upgrading as soon as you are ready. That does not mean as soon as you have reffed the required

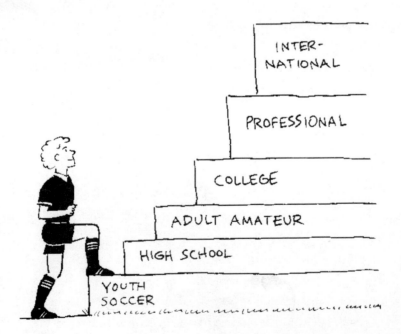

number of games. Ask an older referee whether he thinks you are ready. It's not just a matter of how many games you worked. Do sign up for that assessment when the time comes. Ideally, you should reach the rank of State Referee 1 before age thirty, for there is not all that much time to get to the top. The last few steps to the dizzying heights of National Referee and FIFA are tough ones and take time. FIFA referees have to step down when they turn 46.

12. Whatever level you work at, remain humble. Without a good sense of proportion you will never reach the top in the first place. There is no such thing as a perfect game. Just as in real life, you can only keep learning. And if you love the game, that will be your reward.

So there it is: You are in the game to judge well and to be just and fair on and off the field at whatever level you attain. There will be many opportunities to move up. The new three-tier organization of professional soccer in America sanctioned by the USSF and FIFA is giving soccer a big boost. Play is improving everywhere, and with the prospect of better assignments and pay, so will refereeing. More professional soccer games are being shown on TV, and we should learn from watching the best referees as well as the best players. We must do all we can to recruit and train new referees, both men and women, to meet the challenge.

Soccer is growing — Let us grow with it!

In December 1963, association football or "soccer" became a distinct game. Fourteen laws were adopted in Cambridge to establish the basis of today's game. The field was to be 100 x 200 yards maximum. The kickoff would be taken by the team winning the toss, with the opponents at a ten-yard distance. Goals could not be scored by the ball being thrown or carried. There was an offside rule. The only distinct remnant of the earlier game was the fair catch that entitled a player to punt the ball between the goalposts. The final six rules were crucial: No player could run with the ball. Tripping, hacking, holding, and pushing were not allowed. The ball could not be thrown or passed, except after a fair catch. The final law stated: "No player shall be allowed to wear projecting nails, iron plates or gutta percha on the soles or heels of his boots."

12

BALBOA

Looking Forward

O UR CONSTANT EMPHASIS THROUGHOUT THIS BOOK has been that referees are totally involved in the future of soccer in America. That future has taken on new dimensions in the last few years.

For me, the 1994 World Cup held in the United Sates was a celebration of the new life of soccer in this country. Americans proved again that they love to organize a good party and invite strangers. It was a feast for all of us, Americans as well as thousands of visitors from the corners of the earth. They turned up in large numbers in stadiums all over the

country with their flags, their colorful clothes, and different languages. In this international setting the home team showed that it could play an exciting brand of soccer with respectable results. Soccer appears to have a bright future among us at all levels of play, from young kids to seasoned professionals.

Professional Soccer

The new organization of professional soccer in North America raises a lot of questions about what lies ahead. Will professional soccer be able to compete directly and successfully in the sports market with the Big Four of baseball, football, basketball, and ice hockey? Should that be our goal or should we concentrate our efforts instead on the broadest development of soccer at the amateur level? Will we be able to attract to soccer the athletic talents from a broader economic and social spectrum than we do at present?

There are also questions of spectator appeal for a new soccer public that will not be satisfied with the predominant low scores at the highest level, especially in international tournaments. For America, this might dictate the experimentation with point systems, the size of goals, or the "short corner" free kick that is already going on. Another problem is how to decide games that end in a tie after the usual thirty minutes of overtime. We cannot live much longer with the scandal of frequent penalty-kick shootouts to decide World Cup finals and other top-level competitions.

In Chapter 11 we also discussed the implications for referees. We will have to train a much larger number of outstanding referees for professional soccer. There will be more questions about pay scales in a huge country where interstate travel will require a lot of time of people for whom refereeing is an avocation. And with the rapid rise of women's soccer there will be a need for many more women referees.

My Referee's Wish List

There is much that binds us referees together. Foremost, of course, is our love of the game. Then there are the pleasures and stresses that only we can share as we ply our trade. Not least is our awareness of the mission to serve as best we can the game and the people who play it. That mission goes beyond what we do on the field of play.

Seeking a Larger Voice

Most of us do our job without playing an active role in planning the future of soccer in this country and across the world. That is a pity. Referees have much to contribute outside the field of play. We know the game from the inside. We are trained to be objective and coolheaded. Also, we deal regularly with all the constituencies that make up the soccer community: players from different age groups, genders, and ethnic groups, as well as coaches, spectators, and administrators of large areas.

The views of referees should be welcomed and even solicited by the various governing bodies of soccer when it comes to such things as revising the *Laws of the Game*, the prevention of injuries, dealing with safety and security issues, taking measures to foster racial and gender equality, and the disciplining of players and teams that habitually violate the standards of good sportsmanship. Not least is the question of how to enforce our own codes of integrity and responsibility. I daresay that such initiatives for a more active role would be well received. The talk about redefining our role as a constituent part of soccer has to start among ourselves, however.

Discipline

Whenever there is evidence of serious misconduct by referees, either during games or in the larger society, the local or state association of referees should be involved in whatever action the overseeing boards may take for the good of the game. The USSF's *Referee Administrative Handbook* contains both the "Code of Ethics for Referees" and the "Ethics and Grievance Procedure for Referees, Administrators, Assignors, Instructors, and Assessors." Referees should consult these documents whenever a formal complaint is filed.

Referees may also be involved in actions brought against players, coaches, or referees as a result of particular instances such as acts of violence and assault, game protests brought because of technical referee errors that influenced a game, or the termination of games. We live in a society in which litigation to right alleged wrongs is widespread. Not only in courts of law but also in social institutions of almost any kind that are self-governed, the most elaborate procedures exist to lodge protests and to settle disputes fairly and equitably. That can place a considerable burden on us all.

Many hours are regularly spent in disciplinary board sessions involving elected board members, club officials, players, parents, and referees before a verdict is rendered, and even such verdicts can be appealed. Some referees have been required to travel hundreds of miles to appear before such boards as witnesses to elaborate on their game reports or to

defend their actions. I have occasionally been struck by the readiness with which disciplinary boards are inclined to penalize referees for relatively minor technical errors. In a recent case, a referee who had ejected an abusive coach was disciplined for not having allowed the coach the full two minutes to which he was entitled

before leaving the premises. Here the roles of accuser and accused were clearly reversed, when common sense should have prevailed. The incident had occurred in a game for eleven-year-olds.

My concern is not just the occasional injustice itself, but also the effect of such hearings on our efforts to keep the referees we have and to recruit others. Referees do important volunteer work, requiring substantial talents of head and heart as well as conditioning, for which they are remunerated at modest rates. Referees' abilities and responsibilities far exceed the financial rewards. We should recognize that referees are a valuable resource that must be handled with some care and consideration.

The Consistency Problem

Among the questions raised every four years around World Cup time is the problem of achieving an internationally unified understanding and application of the *Laws of the Game*. How can we get the consistency that is required for international competition? It is not enough for FIFA to gather the referees selected for the World Cup or the Olympics a couple of weeks before the event, test their knowledge and fitness, and give them a few guidelines about calling offsides, protecting goalkeepers, and penalizing certain fouls. First of all, most prominent referees have strong personalities. Many of them hold positions of responsibility in their chosen professions, and they have already achieved distinguished careers as referees at home and abroad. Such people are not suddenly going to change their ways of calling a game because FIFA's referees' committee instructs them to do so. There are still other factors.

Countries and cultures have their own ways of viewing and doing things, whether it is in running households, corporations, or sports asso-

ciations. That is particularly true in handling human relationships involving questions of authority and freedom of choice. In all countries, sports are organized in ways reflecting local attitudes. Sports are played differently — and also refereed differently. In China, as my friend Weidou Xu, a national referee before coming to the U.S., told me a few years ago, a player in offside position is still apt to be routinely flagged the moment there is a forward pass in his general direction. A Chinese referee or linesman is not going to change his acquired habits the moment he comes to Europe. A Mexican referee will deal differently with dissent than a Swede. In a women's game, a male referee from Saudi Arabia may have a different view of what constitutes a legal tackle than his female colleague from the United States. When a British referee has grown up with very sturdy fullback play in rain and mud à la Nobby Stiles, he is unlikely to change his standards of tackling when confronted with a light-footed fancy forward like Maradona in the Argentine sunshine. And so on . . . .

In my view, these more or less ingrained habits are a problem only if we insist on worldwide uniformity in every regard. Just as players have their own styles of playing, so do referees differ in their styles of refereeing, whether those styles are personal or cultural. In one sense, the Olympic Games and the World Cup are celebrations of diversity. The important thing is that we come together to have great international sports encounters that demonstrate and celebrate these differences while at the same time highlighting all that we have in common. Nonetheless, there are things that can be done to promote consistency. FIFA could prepare its referees at least a year in advance by singling out a few important issues for discussion in regional or national conferences, with at least one veteran FIFA referee from another continent present. The benefits could be significant.

I also think that we should do on a smaller scale what I have suggested for FIFA: to cross borders and oceans to let referees from different countries work together on less weighty occasions. Dozens of youth teams from the U.S. play in vacation tournaments in Europe every year. Why can't referees do the same: work out exchanges with referees from other countries during their vacations? It doesn't have to be with Europe. Mexico and Costa Rica, for example, are closer and cheaper. The respective referee associations should be able to arrange for assignments back and forth during the summer, as well as for lodging and meals with referees in the country one visits. On a still smaller scale, such arrangements should also work closer to home, for example at USYSA regional play-off tournaments.

A FINAL CALL

In most countries around the world, referees work principally at the level to which they are assigned by their associations, based on frequent assessments. In America, with our multiple forms of soccer from professionals and top amateurs to local men's and women's leagues, college and high school soccer, and youth competition from ages eight to eighteen, that is different. Most of us operate on at least three or four levels, with referees of all different levels of experience. It is educational in many ways, but it also requires a great deal of flexibility and a gift for cooperating successfully. That sums up the message and purpose of this book: to help us work together on and off the field to promote soccer as a sport that brings people of all stripes together in fair competition.

A few dates from the modern history of soccer:

1866 The offside rule carried the clause "at the time the ball is played."

1872 The corner kick was introduced, and the size of the ball was standardized.

1876 The goals got crossbars; referees began to use whistles.

1885 The Football Association formally accepted professional soccer.

1891 Referees got linesmen; goals got nets.

1896 The term "intentional" appeared in the rules.

1904 FIFA was founded in Paris by seven European countries. England was absent, and its relationship with the international body remained strained until after World War II.

1940 The first World Cup was held in Uruguay, with the home country beating Argentina in the final game.

1950 The first postwar World Cup was held in Brazil. The U.S. team beat England 1–0. Uruguay beat Brazil for its second championship.

1994 The World Cup was held in the United States.

FIFTY QUESTIONS

The following sample questions test not only your knowledge of the *Laws of the Game* but also their application in situations not specifically covered by the laws. That's why this is not a true-and-false or multiple-choice test. Do think your own answers through carefully before you check them against the answers printed in Appendix III. Some of the questions may appear to you farfetched, and you may disagree with some of my answers, though they have been checked with several USSF instructors. All of the situations they cover have occurred in my experience on the field. Eventually, you will encounter them too, as well as other situations that may be unusual. That's life for a referee — often puzzling but always exciting.

Questions

1. What are the minimum legal dimensions of the playing field? What should the referee do if she finds that the field as marked is too small? What if the penalty area does not have the correct dimensions?

2. Before the start of a game, the referee declares the field unsafe. A league official disagrees and orders the game to be played. What should the referee do? (USSF, college, high school?)

3. Team captain A wins the toss and chooses to defend the north goal. As the referee walks away, the team's coach shouts to the captain that he should have chosen the opposite end of the field. Should the referee allow a change?

4. How should the referee respond when before the start of the game the coach of team A tells him that a player of team B is not eligible to play?

5. Because of inclement weather in a youth game, coaches ask the referee to play each half ten minutes shorter. Should he allow that or possibly suggest a different arrangement?

6. What should the referee do when a player for whom his coach wants to send in a substitute refuses to leave the field?

7. Are (a) movable goals (b) scoring celebrations? (c) face masks allowed?

8. A player on a team that can field only seven players is injured and needs to be attended to off the field. Should the game be suspended or terminated?

9. While an injured player is being treated on the field, a coach calls his team to the sideline for a coaching session. Is this allowed?

10. At game time, one team is complete, while the other team has only seven players present and asks for a delay. What should the referee do?

11. At the check-in, the referee notices that one of the players has an amputated forearm. Should the player be allowed to take throw-ins?

12. Some time after play has started, the referee notices that team A, which is leading 1-0, has twelve players on the field. What should the referee do? What if the goal was scored just before play is resumed?

13. How and where should a game be restarted when the ball becomes deflated? What if the ball bursts upon hitting underneath the crossbar and falls behind the goal line?

14. What should the referee do if he called "advantage" and the player who was fouled manages a shot on goal but does not score?

15. A throw-in is taken incorrectly. Because the ball goes directly to the other team, the referee calls "play on." OK?

16. An indirect free kick is deflected off a defensive player positioned in the wall, and goes into the goal. Does the referee signal "goal"?

17. A player taking a free kick just outside her own penalty area kicks it back to her keeper who is not paying attention. The ball goes directly into the goal. Does it count? If not, how should play be resumed?

18. A clearing kick by team A's defense deflects off the referee in front of the feet of an opposing player who kicks it into the goal. What's the referee's decision?

19. A team's goalkeeper makes a save and punts the ball directly into the opponents' goal. Does it count?

20. The goalkeeper stops a ball with his feet, dribbles it outside the penalty box, moves back into the box and punts it from his hands. Any ruling?

21. In a tournament, a team features a throw-in play whereby one player runs behind the back of her teammate who takes the throw, in order to receive the ball in-bounds farther down the line. Is this legal?

22. A young enthusiastic player runs toward an opponent with arms flailing and uttering yahoo cries. What, if anything, should the referee do about it?

23. As a player screens the ball from an opponent without playing it, in order to let the ball roll out-of-bounds, he is charged by the opponent trying to play the ball. Is that legal?

24. A player in offside position whose team is on the attack steps off the field or kneels down to avoid being called offside. Is this legal?

25. A player who tries to dribble the ball through an opening between two defenders finds they "close the gate" on her. Any call?

26. A player taking a throw-in bounces the ball off an opponent's shins so he can proceed to play it himself. Does this require action by the referee? What if the player throws it in his opponent's face?

27. A forward's rush toward the goal on a corner kick carries her over the goal line into the other team's goal. If in the ensuing action her teammate passes the ball into the goal mouth, should she be called offside?

28. The goalkeeper goes outside the penalty area to receive a goal kick from his fullback, dribbles the ball back into the box and picks it up to punt it upfield. Is this legal?

29. At the beginning of the second half, the linesman erroneously calls team A offside — which is not an uncommon occurrence — and the referee whistles the play dead. Apologies all around, but how is the game to be restarted?

30. While standing on the line marking the penalty area, the goalkeeper reaches outside to grab the ball away from an oncoming opponent. What call would you make?

31. Team A's goalkeeper and a fellow player switch shirts without notifying the referee. The referee does not become aware of the switch until he awards team B a direct kick just outside the penalty area. What does he rule?

32. In the same situation above, the referee becomes aware of the switch only when team A's former goalkeeper scores a goal. Now what does he do?

33. When a player from team A is called for a handling foul and shouts "I never touched it!," the referee just makes a shushing gesture and has the free kick taken. Moments later, a player from team B in a similar situation shouts: "What kind of a [bleeping] call is that?" The referee cards him. Is he being inconsistent?

34. A fight breaks out on the field and two substitutes enter the field from the bench without becoming directly involved in the fight or its aftermath,

and return to the bench. What's the referee's action?

35. The referee, noticing that a linesman is constantly at odds with the bench and spectators behind him, at half time has the linesmen switch positions. Is that warranted?

36. The referee injures a leg muscle and declares himself unable to continue. How shall the game be resumed?

37. A player who is sitting on the ground inside his own penalty area to put on a lost boot sees the ball being directed toward his own goal and throws his boot at it, thus keeping the ball from entering the goal. What is the penalty to the player, what to his team?

38. After an inadvertent whistle, the referee restarts the game with a drop ball on the edge of the goal area. Several defenders gather around the spot of the drop ball, whereupon some attacking players try to muscle in, and a shoving match ensues. What should the referee do?

39. In a free kick situation, while the referee is motioning the defenders' wall back ten yards, the kick is taken and scores. What is the proper decision? What if the kick did not score?

40. In a melee of players in front of the goal, the ball is bounced back and forth in close quarters, touching a few arms. The linesman waves his flag for a foul. The referee, who is in a good position to watch the action, waves him off to let the situation resolve itself. When the linesman persists, the referee waits until the ball is cleared, a goal is scored, or the ball crosses the goal line, before he approaches the linesman. The linesman says he saw a hands violation by the defense. What should the referee do?

41. Three weeks after a difficult game in which he had to caution several players from team A, the referee is assigned to a game involving the same team. A player from team A approaches him before the game, saying "Oh, you again? We're not going to take any [bleep] from you this time!" How should the referee react?

42. A player who is being substituted shouts profanities at the referee as he is leaving the field. What should the referee do? Can the substitute come on?

43. A player spits at an opponent in his own penalty area. What should the referee do? What if the same thing happens right after the halftime whistle? Does he allow a replacement?

44. A goalkeeper shows his anger when the opponents are awarded a penalty kick by refusing to take his place on the goal line. The referee finally allows the kick to be taken without a goalkeeper in place. Is that correct?

45. During the taking of a penalty kick, a teammate of the kicker encroaches before the ball is kicked. The kick does not score. What's the proper decision?

46. During a shoot-out from the penalty mark, team A's goalkeeper hurts her shoulder while diving into a corner. For the next round, team A sends in a substitute goalkeeper. Should the referee allow that?

47. Before the taking of penalty kicks to decide a tied game, team A wins the toss. Its captain announces that his team wants to kick second. Is that a problem?

48. A penalty kick is taken. The ball hits underneath the crossbar and bounces off the goalkeeper's back and into the goal. Goal?

49. What should the referee do if it becomes too dark before the taking of penalty kicks can be completed?

50. When the game is over, several players from the home team that lost the game accost the referee with insulting remarks and threatening gestures. Players of the visiting team escort the referee to his car. One linesman stays behind to quiet down the bellicose players. Is this just "one of those things?"

Appendix II

FIFA
LAWS OF THE GAME

LAW I
The Field of Play

(1) **Dimension.** The field of play shall be rectangular, its length being not more than 130 yards nor less than 100 yards and its breadth not more than 100 yards nor less than 50 yards. (In international matches the length shall be not more than 120 yards nor less than 110 yards and the breadth not more than 80 yards nor less than 70 yards.) The length shall in all cases exceed the breadth.

(2) **Marking.** The field of play shall be marked with distinctive lines, not more than 5 inches in width (not by a V-shaped rut) in accordance with the plan, the longer boundary lines being called the touch-lines and the shorter the goal-lines. A flag on a post not less than 5 ft. high and having a non-pointed top, shall be placed at each corner; a similar flag-post may be placed opposite the half-way line on each side of the field of play, not less than 1 yard outside the touch-line. A halfway-line shall be marked out across the field of play. The center of the field of play shall be indicated by a suitable mark and a circle with a 10 yards radius shall be marked round it.

(3) **The Goal-Area.** At each end of the field of play two lines shall be drawn at right-angles to the goal-line, 6 yards from each goal-post. These shall extend into the field of play for a distance of 6 yards and shall be joined by a line drawn parallel with the goal-line. Each of the spaces enclosed by these lines and the goal-line shall be called a goal-area.

(4) **The Penalty-Area.** At each end of the field of play two lines shall be drawn at right-angles to the goal-line, 18 yards from each goal-post. These shall extend into the field of play for a distance of 18 yards and shall be joined by a line drawn parallel with the goal-line. Each of the spaces enclosed by these lines and the goal-line shall be called a penalty-area. A suitable mark

shall be made within each penalty-area, 12 yards from the mid-point of the goal-line, measured along an undrawn line at right-angles thereto. These shall be the penalty-kick marks. From each penalty-kick mark an arc of a circle, having a radius of 10 yards, shall be drawn outside the penalty-area.

(5) The Corner-Area. From each corner-flag post a quarter circle, having a radius of 1 yard, shall be drawn inside the field of play.

(6) The Goals. The goals shall be placed on the center of each goal-line and shall consist of two upright posts, equidistant from the corner-flags and a 8 yards apart (inside measurement), joined by a horizontal cross-bar the lower edge of which shall be 8 ft. from the ground.

For safety reasons, the goals, including those which are portable, must be anchored securely to the ground.

The width and depth of the cross-bars shall not exceed 5 inches (12 cm). The goal-posts and the cross-bars shall have the same width.

Nets may be attached to the posts, cross-bars and ground behind the goals. They should be appropriately supported and be so placed as to allow the goal-keeper ample room.

Footnote:

Goal nets. The use of nets made of hemp, jute or nylon is permitted. The nylon strings may, however, not be thinner than those made of hemp or jute.

DECISIONS OF THE INTERNATIONAL F.A. BOARD

---

(1) In international matches the dimensions of the field of play shall be: maximum 110 x 75 meters; minimum 100 x 64 meters.

(2) National associations must adhere strictly to these dimensions. Each national association organizing an international match must advise the visiting association, before the match, of the place and the dimensions of the field of play.

[(3) Consists of a table of measurements.]

(4) The goal-line shall be marked the same width as the depth of the goal-posts and the cross-bar, so that the goal-line and goal-posts will conform to the same interior and exterior edges.

(5) The 6 yards (for the outline of the goal-area) and the 18 yards (for the outline of the penalty-area) which have to be measured along the goal-line, must start from the inner sides of the goal-posts.

(6) The space within the inside areas of the field of play includes the width of the lines marking these areas.

(7) All associations shall provide standard equipment, particularly in international matches, when the Laws of the Game must be complied with in every respect and especially with regard to the size of the ball and other equipment which must conform to the regulations. All cases of failure to provide standard equipment must be reported to FIFA.

(8) In a match played under the rules of a competition if the cross-bar becomes displaced or broken, play shall be stopped and the match abandoned unless the cross-bar has been repaired and replaced in position or a new one provided without such being a danger to the players. A rope is not considered to be a satisfactory substitute for a cross-bar.

In a friendly match, by mutual consent, play may be resumed without the cross-bar provided it has been removed and no longer constitutes a danger to the players. In these circumstances, a rope may be used as a substitute for a cross-bar. If a rope is not used and the ball crosses the goal-line at a point which, in the opinion of the referee is below where the cross-bar should have been, he shall award a goal.

The game shall be restarted by the referee dropping the ball at the place where it was when play was stopped, unless it was within the goal-area at that time, in which case it shall be dropped on that part of the goal-area, at the point nearest to where the ball was when play was stopped.

(9) National associations may specify such maximum and minimum dimensions for the cross-bars and goal-posts, within the limits laid down in Law I, as they consider appropriate.

(10) Goal-posts and cross-bars must be made of wood, metal or other approved material as decided from time to time by the International F.A. Board. They may be square, rectangular, round, half-round or elliptical in shape.

Goal-posts and cross-bars made of other materials and in other shapes are not permitted. The goal-posts must be of white color.

(11) Any kind of publicity is forbidden in connection with, or on, the field of play. In particular, no advertising material may be displayed at any level on nets, corner flags or goalposts, nor shall such appurtenances of the game have any extraneous equipment attached to them (cameras, microphones, etc.). The reproduction of a FIFA, Confederation, National Association, League, Club or any other logo on the field of play (turf) is also forbidden.

(12) 'Curtain-raisers' to international matches should only be played following agreement on the day of the match, and taking into account the condition of the field of play, between representatives of the two associations and the referee (of the international match).

(13) National associations, particularly in international matches, should
·   restrict the number of photographers around the field of play,
·   have a line (photographers' line) marked behind the goal-lines at least two meters from the corner flag going through a point situated at least 3.5 meters behind the intersection of the goal-line with the line marking the goal-area to a point situated at least six meters behind the goal-posts,

- prohibit photographers from passing over these lines,
- forbid the use of artificial lighting in the form of "flashlights".

(14) A mark may be made off the field of play, 11 yards from the corner flag and at right angles to the goal-line, to help the referee ensure that this distance is observed when a corner kick is being taken.

LAW II
The Ball

The ball shall be spherical; the outer casing shall be of leather or other approved materials. No material shall be used in its construction which might prove dangerous to the players.

The circumference of the ball shall not be more than 28 in. and not less than 27 in. The weight of the ball at the start of the game shall not be more than 16 oz. nor less than 14 oz. The pressure shall be equal to 0.6-1.1 atmosphere (=600-1,100 gr/cm 2) at sea level. The ball shall not be changed during the game unless authorized by the referee.

DECISIONS OF THE INTERNATIONAL F.A. BOARD

---

(1) The ball used in any match shall be considered the property of the association or club on whose ground the match is played, and at the close of play it must be returned to the referee.

(2) The International Board, from time to time, shall decide what constitutes approved materials. Any approved material shall be certified as such by the International Board.

(3) The Board has approved these equivalents of the weights specified in the Law: 14 to 16 ounces = 396 to 453 grams.

(4) For FIFA competition matches and competition matches under the auspices of the Confederations, only footballs which have been tested and which have been shown to meet the minimum technical requirements set forth in Law II, shall be permitted for use. Acceptance of a football for use in the above-mentioned competitions will be conditional upon the football bearing one of the following designations to indicate that it has met the minimal technical requirements:

- The official "FIFA APPROVED" logo
- The official "FIFA INSPECTED" logo
- The reference "International Matchball Standards" (together with other such indications of technical conformity, as requested by FIFA).

In all other matches the ball used must satisfy the requirements of Law II. National Associations or Competitions may require the use only of balls bearing one of the aforementioned designations.

(5) If the ball bursts or becomes deflated during the course of a match, the game shall be stopped and restarted by dropping the new ball at the place where the first ball became defective, unless it was within the goal-area at that time, in which case it shall be dropped on that part of the goal-area which runs parallel to the goal-line, at the point nearest to where the ball was when play was stopped.

(6) If this happens during a stoppage of the game (place-kick, goal-kick, corner-kick, free-kick, penalty-kick or throw-in), the game shall be restarted accordingly.

[*Abbreviated*]

LAW III
Number of Players

(1) A match shall be played by two teams, each consisting of not more than eleven players, one of whom shall be the goalkeeper.

(2) Up to a maximum of three substitutes may be used in any match played in an official competition under the auspices of FIFA, the Confederations or the National Associations.

The rules of the competition shall state how many substitutes may be nominated, from three up to a maximum of seven.

The names of the substitutes must be given to the referee prior to the commencement of the match.

Substitutes not so names may not take part in the match.

(3) In other matches, up to five substitutes may also be used provided that the teams concerned reach an agreement on a maximum number, and that the referee is informed before the match. If the referee is not informed, or no agreement is reached before the commencement of the match, no more than three substitutes shall be permitted.

The names of the substitutes must be given to the referee prior to the commencement of the match.

(4) Any of the other players may change places with the goalkeeper, provided that the referee is informed before the change is made, and provided also that the change is made during a stoppage of the game.

(5) When a goalkeeper or any other player is to be replaced by a substitute, the following conditions shall be observed:

(a) The referee shall be informed of the proposed substitution, before it is made.

(b) The substitute shall not enter the field of play until the player he is replacing has left, and then only after having received a signal from the referee.

(c) he shall enter the field during a stoppage in the game, and at the halfway line.

(d) A player who has been replaced shall not take any further part in the game.

(e) A substitute shall be subject to the authority and jurisdiction of the referee whether called upon to play or not.

(f) The substitution is completed when the substitute enters the field of play, from which moment he becomes a player and the player whom he is replacing ceases to be a player.

Punishment:

(a) Play shall not be stopped for an infringement of paragraph 4. The players concerned shall be cautioned immediately the ball goes out of play.

(b) If a substitute enters the field of play without the authority of the referee, play shall be stopped. The substitute shall be cautioned and removed from the field or sent off according to the circumstances. The game shall be restarted by the referee dropping the ball at the place where it was when play was stopped, unless it was within the goal-area at that time, in which case it shall be dropped on that part of the goal-area line which runs parallel to the goal-line, at the point nearest to where the ball was when play was stopped.

(c) For any other infringement of this Law, the player concerned shall be cautioned, and if the game is stopped by the referee to administer the caution, it shall be restarted by an indirect free-kick, to be taken by a player of the opposing team from the place where the ball was when play was stopped, subject to the overriding conditions imposed in Law XIII.

DECISIONS OF THE INTERNATIONAL F.A. BOARD

(1) The minimum number of players in a team is left to the discussion of national associations.

(2) The Board is of the opinion that a match should not be considered valid if there are fewer than seven players in either of the teams.

(3) A player who has been ordered off before play begins may only be replaced by one of the named substitutes. The kick-off must not be delayed to allow the substitute to join his team.

A player who has been ordered off after play has started may not be replaced.

A named substitute who has been ordered off, either before or after play has started, may not be replaced.

(This decision only relates to players who are ordered off under Law XII. It does not apply to players who have infringed Law IV.)

LAW IV
Players' Equipment

(1) (a) The basic compulsory equipment of a player shall consist of a jersey or shirt, shorts, stockings, shinguards and footwear.

(b) A player shall not wear anything which is dangerous to another player.

(2) Shinguards, which must be covered entirely by the stocking, shall be made of a suitable material (rubber, plastic, polyurethane or similar substance) and shall afford a reasonable degree of protection.

(3) The goalkeeper shall wear colors which distinguish him from the other players and from the referee.

Punishment:

For any infringement of this Law, the player at fault shall be instructed to leave the field of play by the referee, to adjust his equipment or obtain any missing equipment, when the ball next ceases to be in play, unless by then the player has already corrected his equipment. Play shall not be stopped immediately for an infringement of this Law. A player who is instructed to leave the field to adjust his equipment or obtain missing equipment shall not return without first reporting to the referee, who shall satisfy himself that the player's equipment is in order. The player shall only re-enter the game at a moment when the ball has ceased to be in play.

DECISIONS OF THE INTERNATIONAL F.A. BOARD

---

(1) In international matches, international competitions, international club competitions and friendly matches between clubs of different national associations, the referee, prior to the start of the game, shall inspect the player's equipment and prevent any player whose equipment does not conform to the requirements of this Law from playing until such time as it does comply. The rules of any competition may include a similar provision.

(2) If the referee finds that a player is wearing articles not permitted by the Laws and which may constitute a danger to other players, he shall order him to take them off. If he

fails to carry out the referee's instruction, the player shall not take part in the match.

(3) a player who has been prevented from taking part in the game or a player who has been sent off the field for infringing Law IV must report to the referee during a stoppage of the game and may not enter or re-enter the field of play unless and until the referee has satisfied himself that the player is no longer infringing Law IV.

(4) A player who has been prevented from taking part in a game or who has been sent off because of an infringement of Law IV, and who enters or re-enters the field of play to join or re-join his team, in breach of the conditions of Law XII (j) shall be cautioned.

If the referee stops the game to administer the caution, the game shall be restarted by an indirect free-kick, taken by a player of the opposing side, from the place where the ball was when the referee stopped the game, subject to the overriding conditions imposed in Law XIII.

LAW V
Referees

A referee shall be appointed to officiate in each game. His authority and the exercise of the powers granted to him by the Laws of the Game commence as soon as he enters the field of play.

His power of penalizing shall extend to offenses committed when play has been temporarily suspended, or when the ball is out of play. His decision on points of fact connected with the play shall be final, so far as the result of the game is concerned. He shall:

(a) enforce the Laws.

(b) refrain from penalizing in cases where he is satisfied that, by doing so, he would be giving an advantage to the offending team.

(c) keep a record of the game; act as timekeeper and allow the full or agreed time, adding thereto all time lost through accident or other cause.

(d) have discretionary power to stop the game for an infringement of the Laws and to suspend or terminate the game whenever, by reason of the elements, interference by spectators, or other cause, he deems such stoppage necessary. In such a case he shall submit a detailed report to the competent authority, within the stipulated time, and in accordance with the provisions set up by the National Association under whose jurisdiction the match was played. Reports will be deemed to be made when received in the ordinary course of post.

(e) from the time he enters the field of play, caution and show a yellow card to any player guilty of misconduct or ungentlemanly behavior. In such cases the referee shall send the name of the offender to the competent authority, within the stipulated time, and in accordance with the provisions set up by the national association under whose jurisdiction the match was played.

(f) allow no person other than the players and assistant referees to enter the field of play without his permission.

(g) stop the game if, in his opinion, a player has been seriously injured; have the player removed as soon as possible from the field of play, and immediately resume the game. If a player is slightly injured, the game shall not be stopped until the ball has ceased to be in play. A player who is able to go to the touch- or goal-line for attention of any kind, shall not be treated on the field of play.

(h) send off the field of play and show a red card to any player who, in his opinion, is guilty of violent conduct, serious foul play, the use of foul or abusive language, or is guilty of a second cautionable offense.

(i) signal for recommencement of the game after all stoppages.

(j) decide that the ball provided for a match meets with the requirements of Law II.

DECISIONS OF THE INTERNATIONAL F.A. BOARD

---

(1) Referees in international matches shall wear a blazer or blouse the color of which is distinct from the colors worn by the contesting teams.

(2) Referees for international matches will be selected from a neutral country unless the countries concerned agree to appoint their own officials.

(3) The referee must be chosen from the official List of International Referees. This need not apply to amateur and youth international matches.

(4) The referee shall report to the appropriate authority misconduct or any misdemeanor on the part of spectators, officials, players, named substitutes or other persons which take place either on the field of play or in its vicinity at any time prior to, during, or after the match in question so that appropriate action can be taken by the authority concerned.

(5) Assistant referees are assistants of the referee. In no case shall the referee consider the intervention of an assistant referee if he himself has seen the incident and from his position on the field, is better able to judge. With this reserve, and the assistant referee neutral, the referee can consider the intervention, and if the information of the assistant referee applies to that phase of the game immediately before the scoring of a goal, the referee may act thereon and cancel the goal.

(6) The referee, however, can only reverse his first decision so long as the game has not been restarted.

(7) If the referee applies the advantage clause and the advantage which was anticipated does not develop at that time, the referee shall penalize the original offense.

(8) The Laws of the Game are intended to provide that games should be played with as little interference as possible, and in this view it is the duty of referees to penalize only deliberate breaches of the Law. Constant whistling for trifling and doubtful breaches produces bad feeling and loss of temper on the part of the players and spoils the pleasure of spectators.

(9) By par. (d) of Law V the referee is empowered to terminate a match in the event of grave disorder, but he has no power or right to decide, in such event, that either team is disqualified and thereby the loser of the match. He must send a detailed report to the proper authority who alone has power to deal further with this matter.

(10) If a player commits two infringements of a different nature at the same time, the referee shall punish the more serious offense.

(11) It is the duty of the referee to act upon the information of neutral assistant referees with regard to incidents that do not come under the personal notice of the referee.

(12) The referee shall not allow any person to enter the field until play has stopped, and only then if he has given him a signal to do so.

(13) A referee (or where applicable an assistant referee or fourth official) shall not be held liable for (1) any kind of injury suffered by a player, official or spectator, (2) any damage to property of any kind, or (3) any other loss suffered by any individual, club, company, association or similar body, due or which may be due to any decision which he may take in terms of the Laws of the Game or in respect of the normal procedures required to hold, play and control a match.

Such a decision may be

(a) a decision that the condition of the field of play or its surrounds or that the weather conditions are such as to allow or not to allow a match to take place,

(b) a decision to abandon a match for whatever reason,

(c) a decision as to the condition of the fixtures or equipment used during a match including the goal-posts, cross-bar, corner-posts and the ball,

(d) a decision to stop or not to stop a match due to spectator interference or any problem in the spectator area,

(e) a decision to stop or not to stop play to allow an injured player to be treated,

(f) a decision to request or insist that an injured player be removed from the field of play for treatment,

(g) a decision to allow or not to allow a player to wear certain apparel or equipment,

(h) a decision (in so far as this may be his responsibility) to allow or not to allow any persons (including team or stadium officials, security officers, photographers or other media representatives) to be present in the vicinity of the field of play,

(i) any other decision which he may take in accordance with the Laws of the Game or in conformity with his duties in terms of the Federation, Association or League Rules or Regulations under which the match is played.

(14) The coach may convey tactical instructions to players during the match.

The coach and other officials, however, must remain within the confines of the technical area, where such an area is provided and they must conduct themselves, at all times, in a responsible manner.

(15) In tournaments or competitions where a fourth official is appointed, his role and duties shall be in accordance with the guide-lines approved by the International Football Association Board.

LAW VI
Assistant Referees

Two assistant referees shall be appointed, whose duty (subject to the decision of the referee) shall be to indicate:

(a) when the ball is out of play,

(b) which side is entitled to a corner-kick, goal-kick or throw-in,

(c) when a player may be penalized for being in an offside position;

(d) when misconduct or other incident has occurred out of the vision of the referee;

(e) when a substitute is desired.

They shall also assist the referee to control the game in accordance with the Laws. In the event of undue interference or improper conduct by an assistant referee, the referee shall dispense with his services and arrange for a substitute to be appointed. (The matter shall be reported by the referee to the competent authority.)

The assistant referees should be equipped with flags by the club on whose ground the match is played.

DECISIONS OF THE INTERNATIONAL F.A. BOARD

---

(1) Assistant referees, where neutral, shall draw the referee's attention to any breach of the Laws of the Game of which they become aware if they consider that the referee may not have seen it, but the referee shall always be the judge of the decision to be taken.

(2) In international "A" matches, national associations should appoint neutral assistant referees from the International List.

(3) In international matches assistant referee's flags shall be of a vivid color, bright reds and yellows. Such flags are recommended for use in all other matches.

(4) An assistant referee may be subject to disciplinary action only upon a report of the referee for unjustified interference or insufficient assistance.

LAW VII
Duration of the Game

The duration of the game shall be two equal periods of 45 minutes, unless otherwise mutually agreed upon, subject to the following:
(a) Allowance shall be made in either period for all time lost through substitution, the transport from the field of injured players, time-wasting or other case, the amount of which shall be a matter for the discretion of the referee.
(b) Time shall be extended to permit a penalty-kick being taken at or after the expiration of the normal period in either half.

The half-time interval shall not exceed fifteen minutes.

Competition rules shall clearly stipulate the duration of the half-time interval.

The duration of the half-time interval may be altered only with the consent of the referee.

DECISION OF THE INTERNATIONAL F.A. BOARD

---

(1) If a match has been stopped by the referee, before the completion of the time specified in the rules, for any reason stated in Law V, it must be replayed in full unless the rules of the competition concerned provide for the result of the match at the time of such stoppage to stand.
(2) Players have a right to an interval at half-time.

LAW VIII
The Start of Play

(a) **At the beginning of the game,** choice of ends and the kick-off shall be decided by the toss of a coin. The team winning the toss shall have the option of choice of ends or the kick-off. The referee having given a signal, the game shall be started by a player taking a place-kick (i.e. a kick at the ball while it is stationary on the ground in the center of the field of play) into his opponents' half of the field of play. Every player shall be in his own half of the field and every player of the team opposing that of the kicker shall remain not less than 10 yards from the ball until it is kicked-off; it shall not be deemed in play until it has travelled the distance of its own circumference. The kicker shall not play the ball a second time until it has been touched or played by another player.

(b) **After a goal has been scored,** the game shall be restarted in like manner by a player of the team losing the goal.

(c) **After half time;** when restarting after half-time, ends shall be changed and the kick-off shall be taken by a player of the opposite team to that of the player who started the game.

Punishment:

For any infringement of this Law, the kick-off shall be retaken, except in the case of the kicker playing the ball again before it has been touched or played by another player; for this offense an indirect free-kick shall be taken by a player of the opposing team from the place where the infringement occurred, subject to the overriding conditions imposed in Law XIII.

A goal shall not be scored direct from a kick-off.

(d) **After any other temporary suspension;** when restarting the game after a temporary suspension of play from any cause not mentioned elsewhere in these Laws, provided that immediately prior to the suspension the ball has not passed over the touch-or goal-lines, the referee shall drop the ball at the place where it was when play was suspended, unless it was within the goal-area at that time, in which case it shall be dropped on that part of the goal-area line which runs parallel to the goal-line, at the point nearest to where the ball was when play was stopped. it shall be deemed in play when it has touched the ground; if, however, it goes over the touch- or goal-lines after it has been dropped by the referee, but before it is touched by a player, the referee shall again drop it. A player shall not play the ball until it has touched the ground.

If this section of the Laws is not complied with, the referee shall again drop the ball.

DECISIONS OF THE INTERNATIONAL F.A. BOARD

(1) If, when the referee drops the ball, a player infringes any of the Laws before the ball has touched the ground, the player concerned shall be cautioned or sent off the field according to the seriousness of the offense, but a free-kick cannot be awarded to the opposing team because the ball was not in play at the time of the offense.

The ball shall therefore be again dropped by the referee.

(2) Kicking-off by persons other than the players competing in a match is prohibited.

LAW IX
Ball in and out of Play

The ball is out of play:
(a) when it has wholly crossed the goal-line or touch-line, whether on the ground or in the air.
(b) when the game has been stopped by the referee.
   The ball is in play at all other times from the start of the match to the finish including:
(a) if it rebounds from a goal-post, cross-bar or corner-flag post into the field of play.
(b) if it rebounds off either the referee or assistant referee when they are in the field of play.
(c) in the event of a supposed infringement of the Laws, until a decision is given.

DECISIONS OF THE INTERNATIONAL F.A. BOARD

---

(1) The lines belong to the areas of which they are the boundaries. In consequence, the touch-lines and the goal-lines belong to the field of play.

LAW X
Method of Scoring

Except as otherwise provided by these Laws, a goal is scored when the whole of the ball has passed over the goal-line, between the goal-posts and under the cross-bar, provided it has not been thrown, carried or intentionally propelled by hand or arm, by a player of the attacking side, except in the case of a goalkeeper, who is within his own penalty-area.
   The team scoring the greater number of goals during a game shall be the winner; if no goals or an equal number of goals are scored, the game shall be termed a "draw."

DECISIONS OF THE INTERNATIONAL F.A. BOARD

---

(1) Law X defines the only method according to which a match is won or drawn; no variation whatsoever can be authorized.

(2) A goal cannot in any case be allowed if the ball has been prevented by some outside agent from passing over the goal-line. If this happens in the normal course of play, other than at the taking of a penalty-kick: the game must be stopped and restarted by the referee dropping the ball at the place where the ball came into contact with the interference, unless ti was within the goal-area at that time, in which case it shall be dropped on that part of the goal-area line which runs parallel to the goal-line, at the point nearest to where the ball was when play was stopped.

(3) If, when the ball is going into goal, a spectator enters the field before it passes wholly over the goal-line and tries to prevent a score, a goal shall be allowed if the ball goes into goal unless the spectator has made contact with the ball or has interfered with play, in which case the referee shall stop the game and restart it by dropping the ball at the place where the contact or interference occurred, unless it was within the goal-area at that time, in which case it shall be dropped on that part of the goal-area line which runs parallel to the goal-line, at the point nearest to where the ball was when play was stopped.

LAW XI
Off-side

1. A player is in an off-side position if he is nearer to his opponents' goal-line than the ball, unless:

(a) he is in his own half of the field of play, or

(b) he is not nearer to his opponents' goal-line than at least two of his opponents.

2. It is not an offense in itself to be in an off-side position

A player shall only be penalized for being in an off-side position if, at the moment the ball touches, or is played by one of his team, he is, in the opinion of the referee, involved in active play by:

(a) interfering with play, or

(b) interfering with an opponent, or

(c) gaining an advantage by being in that position.

3. A player shall not be declared off-side by the referee

(a) merely because of his being in an off-side position, or

(b) if he receives the ball direct from a goal-kick, a corner-kick, or a throw-in.

4. If a player is declared off-side, the referee shall award an indirect free-kick, which shall be taken by a player of the opposing team from the place where the infringement occurred, unless the offense is committed by a player in his opponents' goal area, in which case the free-kick shall be taken from any point within the goal area.

DECISIONS OF THE INTERNATIONAL F.A. BOARD

---

(1) Off-side shall not be judged at the moment the player in question receives the ball, but at the moment when the ball is passed to him by one of his own side. A player who is not in an off-side position when one of his colleagues passes the ball to him or takes a free-kick, does not therefore become off-side if he goes forward during the flight of the ball. (2) A player who is level with the second last opponent or with the last two opponents is not in an off-side position.

LAW XII
Fouls and Misconduct

A player who commits any of the following six offenses in a manner considered by the referee to be careless, reckless or involving disproportionate force:

    (a) kicks or attempts to kick an opponent; or

    (b) trips an opponent; or

    (c) jumps at an opponent; or

    (d) charges an opponent; or

    (e) strikes or attempts to strike an opponent; or

    (f) pushes an opponent;

or who commits any of the following four offenses:

    (g) when tackling an opponent makes contact with the opponent before contact is made with the ball; or

    (h) — holds an opponent or

        — spits at an opponent; or

    (i) handles the ball deliberately, i.e., carries, strikes or propels the ball with his hand or arm (this does not apply to the goalkeeper within his own penalty-area);

    shall be penalized by the award of a **direct free-kick** to be taken by the opposing team from the place where the offense occurred, unless the offense is committed by a player in his opponents' goal-area, in which case the free-kick shall be taken from any point within the goal-area.

Should a player of the defending team commit one of the above ten offenses within the penalty-area, he shall be penalized by a **penalty-kick.**

A penalty-kick can be award irrespective of the position of the ball, if in play, at the time an offense within the penalty-are is committed.

A player committing any of the five following offenses:

1. playing in a manner considered by the referee to be dangerous;

2. charging fairly, i.e. with the shoulder, when the ball is not within playing distance of the players concerned and they are definitely not trying to play it;

3. when not playing the ball, impeding the progress of an opponent, i.e. running between the opponent and the ball, or interposing the body so as to form an obstacle to an opponent;

4. charging the goalkeeper except when he

(a) is holding the ball;

(b) is obstructing an opponent;

(c) has passed outside his goal-area:

5. when playing as a goalkeeper and within his own penalty-area:

(a) from the moment he takes control of the ball with his hands, he takes more than 4 steps in any direction whilst holding, bouncing or throwing the ball in the air and catching it again, without releasing it into play, or

(b) having released the ball into play before, during or after the 4 steps, he touches it again with his hands, before it has been touched or played by a player of the opposing team either inside or outside of the penalty area, or by a player of the same team outside the penalty area, subject to the over-riding conditions of 5(c), or

(c) touches the ball with his hands after it has been deliberately kicked to him by a team-mate, or

(d) indulges in tactics, which in the opinion of the referee, are designed to hold up the game and thus waste time and so give an unfair advantage to his own team., shall be penalized by the award of an **indirect free-kick** to be taken by the opposing side from the place where the infringement occurred, subject to the overriding conditions imposed in Law XIII.

A player shall be **cautioned and shown the yellow card** if:

(j) he enters or re-enters the field of play to join or rejoin his team after the game has commenced, or leaves the field of play during the progress of the game (except through accident) without, in either case, first having received a signal from the referee showing him that he may do so. If the referee stops the game to administer the cation, the game shall be restarted by an indirect free-kick taken by a player of the opposing team from the place where the ball was when the referee stopped the game, subject to the overriding conditions imposed in Law XIII.

If, however, the offending player has committed a more serious offense, he shall be penalized according to that section of the law he infringed.

(k) he persistently infringes the Laws of the Game;

(l) he shows, by word or action, dissent from any decision given by the referee;

(m) he is guilty of ungentlemanly conduct.

For any of these last three offenses, in addition to the caution, an indirect free-kick shall also be awarded to the opposing side from the place where the offense occurred, subject to the overriding conditions imposed in Law XIII, unless a more serious infringement of the Laws of the Game was committed.

A player shall be **sent off the field of play and shown the red card,** if, in the opinion of the referee, he:

(n) is guilty of violent conduct;

(o) is guilty of serious foul play;

(p) uses foul or abusive language;

(q) is guilty of a second cautionable offense after having received a caution.

If play is stopped by reason of a player being ordered from the field for an offense without a separate breach of the Law having been committed, the game shall be resumed by an **indirect free-kick** awarded to the opposing side from the place where the infringement occurred, subject to the overriding conditions imposed in Law XIII.

DECISIONS OF THE INTERNATIONAL F.A. BOARD

(1) If the goalkeeper either strikes an opponent by throwing the ball at him or pushes him with the ball wile still holding it, the referee shall award a penalty-kick, if the offense took place within the penalty-area.

(2) If a player leans on the shoulders of another player of his own team in order to head the ball, the referee shall stop the game, caution the player for ungentlemanly conduct and award an indirect free-kick to the opposing side.

(3) A player's obligation when joining or rejoining his team after the start of the match to re 'report to the referee' must be interpreted as meaning 'to draw the attention of the referee from the touch-line.' The signal from the referee shall be made by a definite gesture which makes the player understand that he may come into the field of play; it is not necessary for the referee to wait until the game is stopped (this does not apply in respect of an infringement of Law IX), but the referee is the sole judge of the moment in which he gives his signal of acknowledgment.

(4) The letter and spirit of Law XII do not oblige the referee to stop a game to administer a caution. He may, if he chooses, apply the advantage. If he does apply the advantage, he shall caution the player when play stops.

(5) If a player covers up the ball without touching it in an endeavor not to have it played by an opponent, he obstructs but does not infringe Law XII par. 3 because he is already in possession of the ball and covers it for tactical reasons whilst the ball remains within playing distance. In fact, he is actually playing the ball and does not commit an infringement; in this case, the player may be charged because he is in fact playing the ball.

(6) If a player positions his arms to impede an opponent and steps from one side to the other, moving his arms up and down to delay his opponent, forcing him to change course, but does not make "bodily contact," the referee shall caution the player for ungentlemanly conduct and award an indirect free-kick.

(7) If a player impedes the progress of the opposing goalkeeper, in an attempt to prevent him from putting the ball into play in accordance with Law XII, 5(a), the referee shall award an indirect free-kick.

(8) If, after a referee has awarded a free-kick, a player protests violently by using abusive or foul language and is sent off the field, the free-kick should not be taken until the player has left the field.

(9) Any player, whether he is within or outside the field of play, whose conduct is ungentlemanly or violent, whether or not it is directed towards an opponent, a colleague, the referee, an assistant referee or other person, or who uses foul or abusive language, is guilty of an offense, and shall be dealt with according to the nature of the offense committed.

(10) If, in the opinion of the referee, a goalkeeper lies on the ball longer than is necessary, he shall be penalized for ungentlemanly conduct and

    (a) be cautioned and an indirect free-kick awarded to the opposing team;

    (b) in case of repetition of the offense, be sent off the field.

(11) The offense of spitting at officials and other person, or similar unseemly behavior shall be considered as violent conduct within the meaning of section (n) of Law XII.

(12) If, when a referee is about to caution a player, and before he has done so, the player commits another offense which merits a caution, the player shall be sent off the field of play.

(13) If, in the opinion of the referee, a player who is moving toward his opponent's goal with an obvious opportunity to score a goal is impeded by an opponent, through unlawful means, i.e. an offense punishable by a free-kick (or a penalty-kick), thus denying the

attacking player's team the aforesaid goal-scoring opportunity, the offending player shall be sent off the field of play for serious foul play in accordance with Law XII (o).

(14) If, in the opinion of the referee, a player, other than the goalkeeper within his own penalty area, denies his opponents a goal, or an obvious goal-scoring opportunity, by intentionally handling the ball, he shall be sent off the field of play for serious foul-play in accordance with Law XII (o).

(15) The International F.A. Board is of the opinion that a goalkeeper, in the circumstances described in Law XII 5(a), will be considered to be in control of the ball by touching it with any part of his hands or arms. Possession of the ball would include the goalkeeper intentionally parrying the ball, but would not include the circumstances were, in the opinion of the referee, the ball rebounds accidentally from the goalkeeper, for example after he has made a save.

(16) Subject to the terms of Law XII, a player may pass the ball to his own goalkeeper using his head or chest or knee, etc. If, however, in the opinion of the referee, a player uses a deliberate trick in order to circumvent article 5(c) of Law XII, the player will be guilty of ungentlemanly conduct and will be punished accordingly under the terms of Law XII; that is to say, the player will be cautioned and shown the yellow card and an indirect free-kick will be awarded to the opposing team from the place where the player committed the offense.

In such circumstances, it is irrelevant whether the goalkeeper subsequently touches the ball with his hands or not. The offense is committed by the player in attempting to circumvent both the text and the spirit of Law XII.

LAW XIII
Free-kick

Free-kicks shall be classified under two headings: "direct" (from which a goal can be scored direct against the offending side), and "indirect" (from which a goal cannot be scored unless the ball has been played or touched by a player other than the kicker before passing through the goal).

When a player is taking a direct or an indirect free-kick inside his own penalty-area, all of the opposing players shall be at least ten yards (9.15 m) from the ball and shall remain outside the penalty-area until the ball has been kicked out of the area. The ball shall be in play immediately it has traveled the distance of its own circumference and is beyond the penalty-area. The goalkeeper shall not receive the ball into his hands, in order that he may thereafter kick it into play. If the ball is not kicked direct into play, beyond the penalty-area, the kick shall be retaken.

When a player is taking a direct or an indirect free-kick outside his own penalty-area, all of the opposing players shall be at least ten yards from the ball, until it is in play, unless they are standing on their own goal-line, between the goal-posts. The ball shall be in play when it has traveled the distance of its own circumference.

If a player of the opposing side encroaches into the penalty-area, or within ten yards of the ball, as the case may be, before a free-kick is taken, the referee shall delay the taking of the kick, until the Law is complied with.

The ball must be stationary when a free-kick is taken, and the kicker shall not play the ball a second time, until it has been touched or played by another player.

Notwithstanding any other reference in these Laws to the point from which a free-kick is to be taken:

1. Any free-kick awarded to the defending team, within its own goal-area, may be taken from any point within the goal-area.

2. Any indirect free-kick awarded to the attacking team within its opponent's goal-area line which runs parallel to the goal-line, at the point nearest to where the offense was committed.

Punishment:

If the kicker, after taking the free-kick, plays the ball a second time before it has been touched or played by another player, an indirect free-kick shall be taken by a player of the opposing team from the spot where the infringement occurred, unless the offense is committed by a player in his opponent's goal-area, in which case the free-kick shall be taken from any point within the goal-area.

DECISIONS OF THE INTERNATIONAL F.A. BOARD

---

(1) In order to distinguish between a direct and an indirect free-kick, the referee, when he awards an indirect free-kick, shall indicate accordingly by raising an arm above his head. He shall keep his arm in that position until the kick has been taken and retain the signal until the ball has been played or touched by another player or goes out of play.

(2) Players who do not retire to the proper distance when a free-kick is taken must be cautioned and on any repetition be ordered off. It is particularly requested of referees that attempts to delay the taking of a free-kick by encroaching should be treated as serious misconduct.

(3) If, when a free-kick is being taken, any of the players dance about or gesticulate in a

way calculated to distract their opponents, if shall be deemed ungentlemanly conduct for which the offender(s) shall be cautioned.

LAW XIV
Penalty-kick

A penalty-kick shall be taken from the penalty-mark and, when it is being taken, all players with the exception of the player taking the kick, properly identified, and the opposing goalkeeper, shall be within the field of play but outside the penalty-area, at least 10 yards from the penalty mark and must stand behind the penalty mark.

The opposing goalkeeper must stand (without moving his feet) on his own goal-line, between the goal-posts, until the ball is kicked. The player taking the kick must kick the ball forward; he shall not play the ball a second time until it has been touched or played by another player. The ball shall be deemed in play directly it is kicked, i.e. when it has traveled the distance of its circumference. A goal may be scored directly from a penalty-kick. When a penalty-kick is being taken during the normal course of play, or when time has been extended at half-time or full-time to allow a penalty-kick to be taken or retaken, a goal shall not be nullified if, before passing between the posts and under the cross-bar, the ball touches either or both of the goal-posts, or the cross-bar, or the goal-keeper, or any combination of these agencies, providing that no other infringement has occurred.

Punishment:
For any infringement of this Law:
(a) by the defending team, the kick shall be retaken if a goal has not resulted.
(b) by the attacking team other than by the player taking a kick, if a goal is scored it shall be disallowed and the kick retaken.
(c) by the player taking the penalty-kick, committed after the ball is in play, a player of the opposing team shall take an indirect free-kick from the spot where the infringement occurred, subject to the overriding conditions imposed in Law XIII.

DECISIONS OF THE INTERNATIONAL F.A. BOARD

---

(1) When the referee has awarded a penalty-kick, he shall not signal for it to be taken,

until the players have taken up position in accordance with the Law.

(2) (a) If, after the kick has been taken, the ball is stopped in its course towards goal, by an outside agent, the kick shall be retaken.

(b) If, after the kick has been taken, the ball rebounds into play, from the goalkeeper, the cross-bar or a goal-post, and is then stopped in its course by an outside agent, the referee shall stop play and restart it by dropping the ball at the place where it came into contact with the outside agent, unless it was within the goal-area at that time, in which case it shall be dropped on that part of the goal-area line which runs parallel to the goal-line, at the point nearest to where the ball was when play was stopped.

(3) (a) If, after having given the signal for a penalty-kick to be taken, the referee sees that the goalkeeper is not in his right place on the goal-line, he shall, nevertheless, allow the kick to proceed. It shall be retaken, if a goal is not scored.

(b) If, after the referee has given the signal for a penalty-kick to be taken, and before the ball has been kicked, the goal-keeper moves his feet, the referee shall, nevertheless, allow the kick to proceed. It shall be retaken, if a goal is not scored.

(c) If, after the referee has given the signal for a penalty-kick to be taken, and before the ball is in play, a player of the defending team encroaches into the penalty-area, or within ten yards of the penalty-mark, the referee shall, nevertheless, allow the kick to proceed. It shall be retaken, if a goal is not scored.

The player concerned shall be cautioned.

(4)(a) If, when a penalty-kick is being taken, the player taking the kick is guilty of ungentlemanly conduct, the kick, if already taken, shall be retaken, if a goal is scored.

The player concerned shall be cautioned.

(b) If, after the referee has given the signal for a penalty-kick to be taken, and before the ball is in play, a colleague of the player taking the kick encroaches into the penalty-area or within ten yards of the penalty-mark, the referee shall, nevertheless, allow the kick to proceed. If a goal is scored, it shall be disallowed, and the kick retaken.

The players concerned shall be cautioned.

(c) If, in the circumstances described in the foregoing paragraph, the ball rebounds into play from the goalkeeper, the cross-bar or a goal-post, and a goal has not been scored, the referee shall stop the game, caution the player and award an indirect free-kick to the opposing team from the place where the infringement occurred, subject to the overriding conditions imposed in Law XIII.

(5)(a) If, after the referee has given the signal for a penalty-kick to be taken, and before the ball is in play, the goalkeeper moves from his position on the goal-line, or moves his feet, and a colleague of the kicker encroaches into the penalty-area or within 10 yards of the penalty-mark, the kick, if taken, shall be retaken.

The colleague of the kicker shall be cautioned.

(b) If, after the referee has given the signal for a penalty-kick to be taken, and before the ball is in play, a player of each team encroaches into the penalty-area, or within 10 yards of the penalty-mark, the kick, if taken, shall be retaken.

The players concerned shall be cautioned.

(6) When a match is extended, at half-time or full-time, to allow a penalty-kick to be taken or retaken, the extension shall last until the moment that the penalty-kick has been completed, i.e. until the referee has decided whether or not a goal is scored, and the game shall terminate immediately the referee has made his decision.

After the player taking the penalty-kick has put the ball into play, no player other than the defending goalkeeper may play or touch the ball before the kick is complete.

(7) When a penalty-kick is being taken in extended time:

(a) the provisions of all of the foregoing paragraphs, except paragraphs (2) (b) and (4) (c) shall apply in the usual way, and

(b) in the circumstances described in paragraphs (2) (b) and (4)(c) the game shall terminate immediately the ball rebounds from the goalkeeper, the cross-bar or the goal-post.

LAW XV
Throw-in

When the whole of the ball passes over a touch-line, either on the ground or in the air, it shall be thrown in from the point where it crossed the line, in any direction, by a player of the team opposite to that of the player who last touched it. The thrower at the moment of delivering the ball must face the field of play and part of each foot shall be either on the touch-line or on the ground outside the touch-line. The thrower shall use both hands and shall deliver the ball from behind and over his head. The ball shall be in play immediately it enters the field of play, but the thrower shall not again play the ball until it has been touched or played by another player. A goal shall not be scored direct from a throw-in.

Punishment:

(a) If the ball is improperly thrown in, the thrown-in shall be taken by a player of the opposing team.

(b) If the thrower plays the ball a second time before it has been touched or played by another player, an indirect free-kick shall be taken by a player of the opposing team from the place where the infringement occurred, subject to the overriding conditions imposed in Law XIII.

DECISIONS OF THE INTERNATIONAL F.A. BOARD

---

(1) If a player taking a throw-in plays the ball a second time by handling it within the

field of play before it has been touched or played by another player, the referee shall award a direct free-kick.

(2) A player taking a throw-in must face the field of play with some part of his body.

(3) If, when a throw-in is being taken, any of the opposing players dance about or gesticulate in a way calculated to distract or impede the thrower, it shall be deemed ungentlemanly conduct, for which the offender(s) shall be cautioned.

(4) A throw-in taken from any position other than the point where the ball passed over the touch-line shall be considered to have been improperly thrown in.

LAW XVI
Goal-kick

When the whole of the ball passes over the goal-line excluding that portion between the goal-posts, either in the air or on the ground, having last been played by one of the attacking team, it shall be kicked direct into play beyond the penalty-area from any point within the goal-area by a player of the defending team. A goalkeeper shall not receive the ball into his hands from a goal-kick in order that he may thereafter kick it into play. If the ball is not kicked beyond the penalty-area, i.e. direct into play, the kick shall be retaken. The kicker shall not play the ball a second time until it has touched or been played by another player. A goal shall not be scored direct from such a kick. Players of the team opposing that of the player taking the goal-kick shall remain outside the penalty-area until the ball has been kicked out of the penalty-area.

Punishment:

If a player taking a goal-kick plays the ball a second time after it has passed beyond the penalty-area, but before it has touched or been played by another player, an indirect free-kick shall be awarded to the opposing team, to be taken from the place where the infringement occurred, subject to the overriding conditions imposed in Law XIII.

DECISIONS OF THE INTERNATIONAL F.A. BOARD

---

(1) when a goal-kick has been taken and the player who has kicked the ball touches it again before it has left the penalty-area, the kick has not been taken in accordance with the Law and must be retaken.

LAW XVII
Corner-kick

When the whole of the ball passes over the goal-line, excluding that portion between the goal-posts, either in the air or on the ground, having last been played by one of the defending team, a member of the attacking team shall take a corner-kick, i.e. the whole of the ball shall be placed within the quarter circle at the nearest corner-flagpost, which must not be moved, and it shall be kicked from that position. A goal may be scored direct from such a kick. Players of the team opposing that of the player taking the corner-kick shall not approach within 10 yards of the ball until it is in play, i.e. it has traveled the distance of its own circumference, nor shall the kicker play the ball a second time until it has been touched or played by another player.

Punishment:
(a) If the player who takes the kick plays the ball a second time before it has been touched or played by another player, the referee shall award an indirect free-kick to the opposing team, to be taken from the place where the infringement occurred, subject to the overriding conditions imposed in Law XIII.
(b) For any other infringement the kick shall be retaken.

Appendix III

TEST ANSWERS

1. The minimum dimensions for the playing field are 100 x 50 yards, but the penalty area should be a standard 44 x 18 yards. The referee should inform both coaches and captains of any irregularities, but proceed with the game using the lines as marked, and make note of it in her game report.

2. The referee is the sole judge of safety. If the league official insists and the teams indicate they will play the game, the referee and his assistants should leave the premises and make a report to the league. (Note: According to high school rules, the host institution has jurisdiction before the game starts, but during the game it will always be the referee's choice whether to continue play.)

3. No. The toss is strictly a matter between the referee and the team captains.

4. He should ask the captain of team B if this is true and report the matter to the league even if the alleged ineligible player does not play. The referee cannot disqualify the player, however, unless she did not have a valid pass.

5. The referee can allow this. Since the weather can change, however, an alternative might be to play the first half in regulation time and to use his judgment as to field and weather conditions during the second half.

6. The *Laws* make no provision for this situation. Let play continue and hope that the troubled team manages to resolve the situation peacefully. In a high school game, however, the player can be sent to the sideline.

7. (a) Movable goals should be anchored down in some way to avoid injuries; (b) prolonged or excessive celebrations, like a player removing his shirt and making a victory round in front of the stands, should result in a caution; (c) face masks are not allowed.

8. Under FIFA rules the game should be terminated. High school rules allow for a short delay to allow the injured player to return.

9. Generally, the rules allow a coach to give instructions to individual players while the game is in progress, but whole-team conferences are not consistent with the spirit of the law. Coaches, of course, should stay off the field of play and players cannot leave the field without permission.
High school rules specifically forbid coaching during delays for injuries.

10. Normally, the game should be started at the appointed time. In lower level competition, if league rules allow and the other team agrees, the referee could delay the kickoff for, say, ten minutes. If not, the referee should order both teams to take the field.. Refusal of a team to comply would force the referee to call off the game and to report the matter to the league.

11. The referee should do nothing until she sees the player take a throw-in. It is then up to her to judge whether the movement of the ball is unusual and gives that team an advantage.

12. In both cases, the goal should be allowed. The matter should be reported, however, since the game could be appealed. A referee should always ask his assistants to keep track of numbers during the game, especially after substitutions.

13. The game should be restarted with a drop ball at the place where the ball became deflated. If the ball first hit the crossbar or goal post, the drop ball should be given at the nearest spot on the edge of the goal area.

14. Resume play with a goal kick, or play on if the ball stays in the field of play. The advantage did materialize when the player was able to take the shot.

15. No. The advantage rule applies only to foul situations.

16. Yes. The goal counts because the ball was touched by another player before going in.

17. Corner kick for the opponents. A goal cannot be scored by a team directly from a free kick into its own goal.

18. However unfortunate, it's a goal. The referee is considered part of the playing field.

19. Goal! This would even apply if the keeper threw the ball.

20. No stoppage of play, unless in the referee's judgment the keeper is delaying the game.

21. No. A player who leaves the field of play without permission of the referee — especially as a deceptive move — should be cautioned.

22. The player should be cautioned for ungentlemanly conduct. Indirect kick for the opponents.

23. The charge is permitted as long as it is not violent.

24. This traditional move is legal but no longer necessary. Under recent offside instructions, a player should never be called unless he is actively involved in the play and takes advantage of his offside position.

25. If contact is made, the call could be holding (direct free kick). Often a more reasonable call in this situation is obstruction (indirect kick), especially if it happened in the penalty area.

26. In the first instance, the play is legal. Most players would consider it provocative, however, and it should be discouraged. In the second instance, the player should be sent off for violent play.

27. As long as the player is not interfering with the play while moving back into the goal box or by shouting to her teammates, play should be allowed to go on.

28. Law XVI does not allow the goalkeeper to "receive the ball into his hands from a goal-kick . . ."

29. The game should be restarted with a drop ball at the place where the player was called offside, unless that place was in the goal area, in which case the drop ball is given on the edge of the goal area.

30. The position of the keeper's feet is irrelevant. The question is where the ball was handled, so the decision is a direct free kick just outside the penalty area.

31. Both players should be cautioned. If the referee or his linesman had noticed such a switch being made, the diplomatic thing would have been to ask the players if they were going to advise him of it.

32. The goal stands, and so do the cautions.

33. No. The referee has properly distinguished between a forgivable spontaneous reaction and insulting behavior, i.e. between incidental and flagrant dissent.

34. The two players should be cautioned for entering the field without permission. If they participated in the incident, they should be sent off, of course.

35. Linespersons serve at the referee's pleasure. At halftime, the switch will be less noticeable. The referee has an opportunity to discuss the situation with his colleague, and it can only help the game.

36. The referee should ask the senior linesperson to take over his duties. The new referee will decide whether the original referee is able to take her place on the line or whether she should appoint a club linesperson.

37. The player is sent off for serious foul play, and the opposing team is awarded a penalty kick.

38. This is a delicate situation, since it was caused by the referee team itself. If it's anywhere close to the goal, the referee should drop the ball as soon as possible and as far from the goal as possible, in order to avoid an embarrassing goal. Nowhere in the *Laws* or F.A. Board "Decisions" is it specified that the ball has to be dropped between two opposing players. Under the circumstances, with players crowding in, the best thing is to drop the ball quickly while telling them to stop pushing. Get the ball into play!

39. Regardless of what happened, the kick has to be retaken, since the ball was never officially in play. The referee can avoid this situation by clearly telling the kicking team to wait for a signal.

40. The referee thanks the linesman but asks him to stop signaling as soon as he waves him off. The game is resumed according to the referee's decision, and they should discuss the situation later.

41. He should caution the player right then and there, and probably — especially in high school — inform his coach. Should the referee disqualify the player at this time, his team does not have to play a man short.

42. The player should be sent off, since he was still on the field. He cannot be replaced, but a substitute may come on for still another player.

43. The player should be sent off for violence. Even after the halftime whistle, he was still a player of record and cannot be replaced.

44. The penalty kick cannot be taken until all players, including the goalkeeper, are in their proper positions. The keeper should be cautioned for delaying the game or sent off if he persists. He can then be replaced, though his team must play short.

45. Goal kick, or indirect kick for the defense if the goalkeeper stopped the penalty kick or the ball bounced back from the goal post or cross bar.

46. Under FIFA rules, the team may use a substitute goalkeeper within the total number of substitutes allowed. If not, they must use a player already on the field.

47. The team that wins the toss must kick first. In high school, the captain has a choice, but it is hard to imagine any team wanting to kick second.

48. It's a goal. The PK action is not finished until the ball has no chance of going in.

49. Normally, the game would be decided by a coin toss.

50. First of all, the referee should not get into arguments or counter-threats and accept the escort. As in all games, the team of referees should leave the field together. The matter should be reported because the host club officials did not do their duty in protecting the referee team. The referee must decide whether he should include the numbers and names of some of the players involved, but he certainly should do so if they jostled or hit him or the linesmen, who should write their own reports.